T4-AFY-336

FREE CHURCH UNITY

HISTORY OF THE FREE CHURCH COUNCIL MOVEMENT 1896–1941

by

E. K. H. JORDAN

LUTTERWORTH PRESS

LONDON

ALL RIGHTS RESERVED
First published 1956

132590
261.9
J762

PRINTED IN GREAT BRITAIN BY
THE BOWERING PRESS, PLYMOUTH

To
the unfading memory
of
JOHN WILLIAM JORDAN
(1887–1951)
whose earthly fatherhood made it easy
for me to believe in the Divine

PREFACE

THIS book is based on a more detailed piece of historical research for which the University of Oxford were gracious enough to award the Doctor of Philosophy degree in 1953. For a number of reasons it was not possible to publish the larger story, and the reader is to be congratulated on escaping the mass of historical detail which a comprehensive thesis requires. The picture in this book, however, is substantially complete and I am extremely happy that its publication coincides with the Diamond Jubilee Celebrations of the Free Church Council movement. It is a happy coincidence in my own mind that the celebrations take place in my home city of Liverpool.

The Free Churches are facing grave problems which will call for mighty decisions and sustained courage, and if this book offers any guidance as to how we should proceed, and any inspiration to begin our march, then it will indeed have accomplished that for which it is now sent forth. History is not, as so many imagine, a dead thing, for it is only by looking backward that we dare step forward, and perhaps if the world had listened more to the historian and less to the fashionable and spectacular prophets of our age, then the story of our century might have been very different.

My gratitude is due to Dr. Ernest Payne, General Secretary of the Baptist Union, who supervised my research at Oxford and has since placed me further in his debt by his sustained interest and ready counsel; to the staff of the Federal Council at Tavistock Square for their consistent help; to the Rev. Cecil Northcott of the Lutterworth Press for his wise shepherding of a beginner;

to my good friend Mr. Graham Gibbs of Malvern who, in the midst of a busy life, has found time to read and correct my final manuscript; and to Miss Ruth Hensman and Miss Ann Judson who devoted themselves to the laborious but important task of indexing.

E. K. H. JORDAN

Malvern
September, 1955

CONTENTS

Chapter 1

IN THE VICTORIAN AGE

THE position of the Free Churches in the Victorian Age can best be described as one of considerable expansion and growing emancipation. The ecclesiastical authorities, concerned at the growth of Nonconformity, were, not unnaturally, hostile to any concession which might improve the status and prospects of Dissenters. When the young Queen ascended the throne in 1837 things had begun to look much brighter for Nonconformists. Almost ten years earlier in 1828, the Corporation Act of 1661 and the Test Act of 1673 had been repealed although, significantly enough, not without determined opposition from certain sections of the Upper House. Earlier than that, in 1812, the Conventicle Act of 1664 and the Five Mile Act of 1665 had also been removed from the statute book. At the start of the Victorian Age therefore, these newly won gains and the steady increase in the ranks of the Dissenters tended to produce a virility and aggressiveness which threatened to make short shrift of the specific grievances which still awaited redress. Having tasted the sweets of partial victory Dissenters were in full cry for complete religious equality. The Established Church, in no mood to abandon its traditional primacy, accepted the challenge, and there began the bitter struggle of the Victorian Age. It was "associated with much that was petty and discreditable on both sides"[1] but the advance of Noncon-

[1] Ernest A. Payne, *The Free Church Tradition in the Life of England*, 1944, p. 104.

formity, though constantly harassed and impeded by the forces of monopoly and privilege, was not to be denied, and slowly but surely the desired objectives were captured.

The main battle raged around the question of church rates. A General Convention of Dissenters in 1834, one of the most important and influential assemblies of its kind up to that point, had vigorously demanded the abolition of this grievance, but it was not until 1868, after the agitation had reached serious proportions, that the Church Rate Abolition Bill became law, thus fulfilling Lord John Russell's famous prophecy:

> I know the Dissenters. They carried the Reform Bill . . . the abolition of slavery. . . . Free Trade; and they'll carry the abolition of Church Rates.

The universities of Oxford and Cambridge were opened to Nonconformists and Roman Catholics in 1871, and nine years later the Burials Bill allowed Nonconformists burial in parochial churchyards with funeral services conducted by their own pastors. All these concessions were won by Nonconformists only after strenuous and often bitter resistance on the part of their opponents, and it was only to be expected that in the face of such hostility the Free Churches would draw closer together in order the better to press their claims.

In the Victorian Age therefore we expect to find many examples of concerted action on the part of Nonconformists, and so it was. Various organizations came to birth in order to uphold their rights. "The Society for Promoting Ecclesiastical Knowledge", although founded some eight years before the accession of the Queen, lasted on into the Victorian Age and proved itself to be a creative attempt to establish a literature which would plead the claims of full religious liberty by examining the true nature of the Church. As such it was valuable propaganda for Nonconformity. Again, in 1839, a conference of Dissenters established "The Religious Freedom Society" whose tenets condemned the whole fabric of the Established Church; while the formation of a Church Rate Abolition Society was a further example of the growing tendency of Nonconformity to group together, sometimes with people who were not actually Dissenters, for more effective public action.

Gradually, however, out of these various organizations there emerged a more important one, formed in 1844, and called the British Anti-State Church Association. This body renewed its existence by a system of triennial conferences and although it aimed at embracing all who longed for a separation of Church and State it was substantially Nonconformist in character and personnel. It has been said that "its history as a modern propagandist organization is absolutely unique",[1] and it appears that it could draw effective support from almost all sections of the Dissenting communities. In 1853 it was re-named "The Society for the Liberation of Religion from State Patronage and Control" but it became known merely as "The Liberation Society", and as such has lasted to our own day. As its name suggests, it laboured continually to keep the issue of Disestablishment before the Nonconformist world although it did actually include a certain number of Anglicans amongst its supporters. The measure of its appeal and progress can be seen in the alarm of the Establishment which issued in the formation of Church Defence Societies. It is remarkable that in Dr. Elliott Binns' admirable book, *Religion in the Victorian Era*, only two references, one somewhat contemptuous and the other merely noting Mr. Disraeli's comment on the Society, are found in the whole length of the work. But Lord Derby, after the passing of the Church Rate Abolition Bill, attri-

[1] Skeats and Miall, *The History of the Free Churches of England*, 1891, p. 533.

buted the substantial majority of the government to the energetic activity of this Society, while the Duke of Argyll referred to it as a political force which statesmen could neither ignore nor despise. In general, it was under the auspices of the Liberation Society that most of the Nonconformist struggles for civil and religious rights were fought out.

We must not make the mistake of thinking however that in the Liberation Society, or the like, we are confronted with what we may call a forerunner of the Free Church Council movement, for, as Dr. Elliott Binns reminds us, the basis of all this concerted action on the part of the Free Churches was not primarily religious but lay in the desire for political action. There was at this time no idea of federation, much less of the Free Churches as one Church by virtue of the spiritual principle underlying their dissent. Moreover, even from the political angle, there was nothing approaching complete unity, for the Methodist bodies numbered countless Tories amongst their ranks and were inclined to repudiate the name "Nonconformist". It was only to be expected therefore that the classical Dissenting traditions would view them with a certain amount of suspicion, the more so because of the substantial secessions from the main Methodist body during the middle decades of the century.

None the less, the Liberation Society and other movements along similar lines are interesting from our point of view because they afford illustrations of the fact that Nonconformity was ceasing to be disorganized, albeit gradually, and that the tendency of the age was "socialistic rather than individualistic".[1] This fact was also to be seen in the closer organization of different groups of Nonconformists. For example, the recognition of common interests by the "independent" congregations had led to the forma-

[1] C. Silvester Horne, *Nonconformity in the Nineteenth Century*, 1905, p. 149.

tion of the Baptist Union in 1831 and the formation of the Congregational Union in the same year. Both denominations had made earlier but abortive attempts along the same lines. Both unions were suspect for some time by certain sections within their denominations but, as the century wore on, along with their county associations, both began to win increasing support and acceptance, and in 1865 the Baptist Union felt confident enough to hold regular autumnal, as well as annual, meetings, while in 1881 the Congregational Union held most popular and successful Jubilee celebrations.

That a nobler and more brotherly spirit was abroad in the decade immediately prior to the inception of the Free Church Council movement is evidenced by certain notable events.

In 1886 the Baptist and Congregational unions held joint meetings in the famous City Temple in an atmosphere of exceptional religious enthusiasm and brotherliness.

In 1888, the bishops of the Lambeth Conference followed up their declaration of 1867 by producing the now famous Lambeth Quadrilateral, which laid down, as a basis for corporate reunion, the acceptance of the historic episcopate, Holy Scripture as the rule and standard of faith, the Apostles' and Nicene creeds, and the sacraments of Baptism and the Lord's Supper.

In 1889, Mansfield College, Oxford, was opened as a theological college and a religious home and centre for Nonconformists in the University of Oxford. In his report in 1890, Principal Fairbairn, describing his college as the epitome of living catholicity, declared that amongst its students were members of the Church of England, Baptists, Methodists, Presbyterians, French Protestants and Lutherans, in addition to the main core of Congregationalists.

These events are illustrations of the emergence, however

slowly, of a refreshingly new spirit of fraternity and a new desire for co-operation, so that, as the last decade of the nineteenth century dawned, the opportunity for the Free Churches to turn fraternal feelings into something more positive and practical was waiting to be grasped.

Chapter 2

VISION OF THE FELLOWSHIP

THE Free Church Council movement was once described as an expression of the yearning which had filled Nonconformist hearts for many long years. The movement was certainly no spasmodic phenomenon for it was brought to birth by "many a gracious inspiration, much earnest thought in devout and loving hearts, and many an impulse of the Spirit of God."[1]

The first Free Church Council or Congress as it was first called, came together in Manchester in November, 1892, but the spirit of federation and a genuine desire for it in some form or other had been abroad for some considerable time before this. Any inquiry into actual origins therefore must concern itself with previous attempts of a similar nature. In our discussion of the general background of Nonconformity we have already noticed evidences of concerted action in the Victorian Age, and of a developing fraternal feeling, but we did not examine any evidence which might be said to have a direct kinship with the Free Church Council movement.

Dr. Elliott Binns maintains that the idea of Free Church Federation was first contemplated by John Angell James, the gifted minister of Carrs Lane Congregational Chapel in Birmingham. Certainly there was no subject nearer to James's heart than that of a much closer grouping of Christians, and in his address to the Congregational Union in May, 1842, he envisaged a Protestant Evangelical Union

[1] *The Free Church Federation Movement*, p. 9. (No indicated author.)

of all Christians who belonged to the "voluntary" churches. In July, 1842, he outlined a scheme for a General Protestant Union, which led on to the famous Exeter Hall meeting of 1843, and ultimately to the formation of the Evangelical Alliance in 1846.[1]

1867 is an interesting year, for there seems to have been a definite attempt to initiate a Free Church Congress, the stimulus coming from the Wolverhampton district where the Anglican Church Congress of that year had met. This Congress was bold enough to discuss methods for bringing Nonconformists into union with the Anglican Church, apparently in such a manner that Nonconformists in the area felt constrained to make some reply. Accordingly, a Committee of Dissenting ministers and laymen from the South Staffordshire and Birmingham areas was formed and certain pamphlets were circulated. These events are related in a most interesting letter to *The Freeman* from the Rev. T. G. Horton[2] and Robert Felkin, Chairman and Secretary of the Wolverhampton Nonconformist Committee. In this letter the following significant words appear:

> The impression has become strong that the time has come when the practicability of a Free Church Congress embracing all Evangelical Dissenters should be seriously entertained, so that the various religious, social and political questions may be fully brought before the Nonconformist body. . . . With a view to inaugurate such a Congress, it has been determined to form a Provisional Committee and to bring this subject before the various free religious organizations of the country, to ascertain how far this wish would meet with an affirmative response.[3]

It seems that the necessary affirmative response was not

[1] R. W. Dale, *Life and Letters of John Angell James*, 1861, pp. 396–398.

[2] Father of R. F. Horton. It was during the father's vigorous ministry in Wolverhampton that Queen Street Congregational Chapel was built for him. Later, Charles Berry ministered to this church.

[3] *The Freeman*, November 8, 1867.

forthcoming, for the appeal did not make any widespread impression, but it is important none the less, for it shows that Free Churchmen were beginning to think along these lines and that the soil was being slowly but surely prepared for the events of the last decade of the century.

In 1872, a most important Nonconformist Conference was held in Manchester. It was, up to that point, probably the largest and most representative assembly of Dissenters ever held in Britain. True, this conference was largely concerned with educational and political issues, but it is significant that it was certainly not a Liberation Society meeting, nor could its purpose have been solely political; for Dr. R. W. Dale of Birmingham was present, and he was notoriously averse to the suggestion that the Free Churches, as such, should take action on political issues. In any event, the holding of such a conference indicates that the Free Churches were then beginning to feel the need of conciliar action, and this was again apparent when later in the same year, Baptists, Methodists, Presbyterians and Congregationalists held a meeting to consider the problems connected with the overlapping of their causes.

In October, 1878, the Congregational Union carried a resolution calling upon the Free Churches to confer together on matters connected with the religious condition of England and to try and reach agreement as to joint action in evangelism. Once again, the attempt to gather the conference proved unsuccessful. The moment was not yet ripe, but the desire for co-operation and joint action was becoming increasingly articulate.

For the next twelve years or so there was no striking development, but it is certain that the idea of some united Free Church movement exercised the minds of many Nonconformists. The seeds were growing secretly but vigorously. Many were waiting for a positive and inspiring lead which would transform latent desires and inclinations into reality.

The first definite suggestion of the Free Church Council movement was a signed article contributed to the *Methodist Times* of February 20, 1890, by the Rev. Dr. Guinness Rogers, one of the leading Congregational figures of the day. Prior to this, Dr. Rogers had received a letter from the Rev. Hugh Price Hughes, a prominent Wesleyan and the prophet of social Christianity, who was also editor of the *Methodist Times*, asking him to contribute an article pleading the claims of a Free Church Congress. The article duly appeared under the heading "A Congress of the Free Churches" and it immediately created widespread and enthusiastic interest. Dr. Rogers indicated the great improvement in the relations of the English Nonconformists and the gradual decay of antipathy and jealousy. Why not press this to its logical conclusion? Why not a Free Church Congress meeting every year, not for the purpose of presenting a hostile attitude to its Anglican counterpart, but for the positive furtherance of the Free Church share in the evangelization of England? Dr. Rogers's final words deserve recording. Such a course, he said:

> would be a public development of a Church idea which at present is hardly realized. Wesleyan, Presbyterian, Baptist, Congregationalist, meeting on the same platform not for an interchange of compliments and courtesies but for true Christian fellowship in devotional service and for counsel on common Christian work, would be a striking illustration of a Catholic Church including various sections, each with its own form of development and with its distinctive features of doctrine and ritual but all one in Christ Jesus.

The next issue of the *Methodist Times* published many letters warmly supporting the proposal. John Clifford, F. B. Meyer, Dr. Bowman Stephenson (Methodist), Dr. Townsend (Methodist), Dr. Watts of the Methodist New

Connexion, and Dr. Keen of the Bible Christians were among those who greeted the new idea with alacrity.

The *Methodist Times* had drawn attention to Dr. Rogers's proposal by contrasting the force and influence, altogether out of all proportion to the respective numbers, wielded by the Roman Catholics on the one hand and Nonconformists on the other. The reason for this sorry state of affairs, the article claimed, was that the Catholics were an organized army and the Nonconformists rather like a disorganized mob.

Two years and nine months were to pass between the publication of Dr. Rogers's sentiments and the meeting of the first Free Church Congress in Manchester in November, 1892, but the spirit of the movement had come to birth, and silent but thorough preparations initiated. Ministers' fraternals began to grow in number and influence, and certain Nonconformist councils appeared. These were hardly on the lines of the later Free Church councils, but they were indeed Nonconformist councils—associations of ministers and congregations although without any definite representative basis or official sanction. In 1890 there were about ten such councils in existence, but two years later the number had more than doubled. It was not spectacular progress but it was progress, and it showed that Nonconformists were becoming more and more aware that some form of co-operation was necessary and desirable.

The years 1891 and 1892, moreover, were years in which the impulses towards co-operation found expression in other ways. In the first place, it was in 1891 that a publication appeared with the title, *The Review of the Churches*. This significant venture originated in conversations between Dr. (later Sir) Henry S. Lunn and Mr. (later Sir) Percy W. Bunting. Both these Wesleyans felt the need for a corporate publication which would deal with the life and thought of the different branches of the Church of Christ. The General Editor was Dr. Lunn, while the denominational editors were Dr. Clifford for the Baptists, Dr. Mackennal for the Congregationalists, Archdeacon Farrar for the Anglicans, Dr. Donald Fraser for the Church of Scotland, and Mr. Percy Bunting for the Methodists. The most striking feature of the *Review* was a monthly Round Table Conference, the first of which was entitled "The Reunion of Christendom". It included, as a matter of interest, a gracious contribution from Mr. Gladstone, soon to be Prime Minister for the fourth time. *The Times*, the *British Weekly*, even the *Church Times*, and a letter from the large-minded Cardinal Manning, all testified to the value of this publication. Perhaps more significant than its actual existence was that it led on to the famous Grindelwald conferences on Christian Reunion.[1] Dr. Lunn had conceived the idea of organizing holiday parties abroad, composed of representatives of the various churches, with the intention of combining the delights of scenery with more serious pursuits. In this way he felt sure that much might be done to remove misunderstanding, to discover common ground, to promote united endeavours and thus to foster feelings of mutual esteem and regard. A preliminary conference on a limited scale in January 1892 showed clearly that there were considerable possibilities in convening a larger conference, and this was done in the summer of 1892.

Dr. Lunn tells us[2] of his ambition and audacity at the age of thirty-three in inviting Mr. Gladstone, all the territorial Bishops, and the leaders of Nonconformity to Grindelwald in Switzerland as his guests. Audacious or not, Dr. Lunn's invitations led to the presence at Grindelwald of such personalities as Bishop Perowne of Worcester,

[1] There were two sessions in 1892, in July and September, and further conferences at Grindelwald in 1893 and 1894, and subsequently further discussions in England.

[2] Henry S. Lunn, *Chapters from My Life*, 1918.

Dean Fremantle, Dr. Ryle (later Bishop of Winchester), Dr. Moule, Bishop of Durham, Dr. Chavasse, Bishop of Liverpool, and High Churchmen such as Canon Hammond, Professor Stokes and Mr. Athelstan Riley. Baptists were represented by Dr. Richard Glover and the Rev. C. F. Aked; Congregationalists by Dr. Charles Berry, Dr. R. F. Horton, Dr. Alexander Mackennal and Dr. Joseph Parker; Presbyterians by Dr. Monro Gibson, Professor A. B. Bruce, Professor Lindsay and Dr. Oliver; and Methodists by the Rev. Hugh Price Hughes, Mr. Percy Bunting and the host.

Many lectures and papers were read, and discussions centred in the main on the fourth clause—that dealing with the historic episcopate—of the famous Lambeth Quadrilateral. The fraternal feeling and harmony present in these meetings was demonstrated when the Bishop of Worcester celebrated a joint Communion, an action which, not unnaturally, aroused a storm in Anglican circles back in England. *The Times*, however, after questioning the Bishop's action, admitted that the Grindelwald Conference was a step in the right direction of better understanding and co-operation. Bishop Perowne endorsed this when he said that if no actual step had been taken towards reunion, at least there had taken place a considerable step forward in the matter of Christian charity.

Some space has been devoted to the Grindelwald conversations because, without any doubt, the 1892 sessions greatly helped the movement towards Free Church Federation. Dr. W. B. Selbie[1] goes so far as to say that the outcome was the foundation of the National Free Church Council mainly under the guidance of Hugh Price Hughes, Charles Berry and Alexander Mackennal, who had all been at Grindelwald. Of course, the Grindelwald conver-

[1] W. B. Selbie, "The Prospects of Free Church Federation in England", *The Constructive Quarterly*, V. 20, Dec., 1917.

sations could only be personal exchanges of opinion, but they nevertheless left some important results behind them. They created an atmosphere of interest in the reunion problem and stimulated the desire for closer fellowship, but the most important factor from our point of view was that they clearly showed that any immediate steps towards reunion must of necessity leave the Anglicans out of the reckoning. It was evident that the external link of the Establishment held together men who were, in no other sense, in real fellowship with one another. The Grindelwald episode, therefore, suggested to many of the Free Church leaders that a beginning in the matter of Christian reunion might best be made by first establishing closer relationships between the Free Churches. As Charles Berry saw it, reunion could only come in easy stages, and the early moves seemed clearly to rest with a *rapprochement* of the Free Churches, for their federation seemed immediately possible in so far as they could come together for the defence of their common rights and the removal of disabilities.

It seems certain that amidst the seclusion of the Swiss valleys many informal discussions took place between leaders of influence in the different denominations. James S. Drummond maintains that

> there can be no doubt that the conversations which took place at Grindelwald between Dr. Berry, Hugh Price Hughes, Dr. Monro Gibson and Dr. Mackennal, enabled them to arrive at unanimity at many points, and thus helped greatly in the maturing of the whole movement.[1]

This is supported by Dr. Lunn, who wrote:

> Every point in their plans, which have resulted in the development of so remarkable a work, was thrashed out in detail between the village of Grindelwald and the surrounding glaciers.[2]

[1] and [2] J. S. Drummond, *Charles A. Berry, D.D.*, 1899, p. 112.

Moreover, this is further supported by the evidence of Miss Dorothea Hughes in her story of her father's life,[1] when she refers to the common mind of Hugh Price Hughes and Charles Berry in their Grindelwald conversations. In Dr. Berry, she tells us, her father saw the man who could become the constructive genius of the movement towards federation. Both men were of large and catholic outlook. An annual gathering of Nonconformists for purely consultative and fraternal intercourse was only a small part of their thought about the nature of the proposed federation, as we shall see later.

In the meantime, however, events had been moving back in England. In 1891, Dr. J. B. Paton, the social and educational pioneer of Nottingham, drew up a circular which was sent to every Nonconformist minister in the country, and bearing the signatures of Hugh Price Hughes, John Clifford, R. F. Horton, J. Scott Lidgett, Charles Berry, as well as Dr. Paton himself. Lewis Paton[2] claims that this circular actually initiated the Free Church Council, but the direct move which brought the first congress to birth, came from the Manchester area. Prior to this, however, Mr. Percy Bunting gave a dinner party at his house in Euston Square, London, to which many Free Church leaders were invited.[3] This gathering seems to have expressed a definite feeling in favour of calling a Free Church Congress, and it is probable that Dr. Paton's circular emanated from this group, for he was an intimate friend of Mr. Percy Bunting, and is almost certain to have been present at Euston Square.

The result was that a memorable meeting of Free Church-

[1] Dorothea Price Hughes, *The Life of Hugh Price Hughes*, 1905, p. 442. cf. also R. F. Horton, *Autobiography*, 1917, p. 246.

[2] Lewis Paton, *John Brown Paton*, 1914, p. 190.

[3] I am indebted to the late Rev. Dr. J. Scott Lidgett for this interesting piece of information. He was invited to the gathering being then a rising young Wesleyan minister.

men came together on the afternoon of Monday, January 11, 1892, at the Central Hall in Oldham Street, Manchester. There was a very large attendance representing all denominations, over which Mr. Henry Lee presided. Mr. Percy Bunting's important speech on that occasion deserves brief notice. He indicated the large number of Free Church leaders who had expressed their readiness to co-operate, which augured well for the venture. He hoped that the work of the Congress when it came into being would be altogether positive, and he went on to make it perfectly clear that it was not a case of Free Churchmen assembling to attack the Anglicans, but rather of enabling all the great Evangelical churches, free from State control, to come together in vital fellowship and endeavour. In his judgment, the Congress would have two central pursuits—firstly, to show that the Free Churches were at one in their general conception of the work of Christ; and, secondly, to demonstrate real co-operation in the great religious problems of the contemporary situation.

Finally, two important resolutions were adopted. The first was moved by Dr. Alexander McLaren, the beloved and famed minister of Oxford Road Baptist Chapel in Manchester:

> that in the opinion of this conference, a Congress of representatives of the Free Churches in the United Kingdom would be of great service to all the Churches, and it would be well to hold such a Congress in Manchester in 1892.

Much later in his life Dr. McLaren could say that there were few things he looked back on in his career with more satisfaction than the remembrance of having moved this famous resolution. Addressing the Free Methodist Conference he urged his hearers to give earnest and unstinting support to the great movement:

> You will not be doing your duty as Christian men unless

you cast yourself with earnestness and sympathy into the work.[1]

The second resolution, moved by Mr. Percy Bunting, ensured that the Congress would be constituted not by delegations from the different church bodies but by the personal and individual adhesion of members of the Free Churches. Bunting was astute enough to see that if members came as Free Churchmen primarily and with no denominational badges officially attached to them, a greater experience of unity might be theirs.

Certain Presbyterian and Methodist members of the gathering expressed fears that the Congress might degenerate into nothing more than a Liberation Society platform, dissipating its potential in anti-Anglican epithets, and they sought, unavailingly, to extract a promise that the Congress should not in any way attack the State control of the Anglican Church.

The accusation has often been levelled at the Free Church Council movement that it was anti-Anglican in origin. There is, on a superficial level, enough apparent truth in this statement to warrant an examination of the facts before we turn our attention to the first Free Church Congress.

Dr. Guinness Rogers, in his article, had referred to the abundant evidence that the Established Church was determined to spare no effort for the suppression of Nonconformity. The Rev. C. Silvester Horne claims[2] that the Free Churches came together in the shadow of a great common peril—that of the increasing Romanization of the Church of England. There can be no doubt that the Tractarian movement had changed the character of the Episcopal Church, and had brought forth and encouraged features which had disappeared before the Puritan re-

[1] *Free Church Chronicle*, August, 1900, p. 259.
[2] C. Silvester Horne, *A Popular History of the Free Churches*, 1903, p. 424.

formers. In its early stages the movement had strongly attacked evangelicalism, and had seemed most interested in reintroducing ancient forms and ceremonies. As the years went by, the ritualist party in the Church of England grew in strength and influence; so much so that in 1874 the Public Worship Regulation Bill was passed in order to put down ritualism, as Mr. Disraeli explained it. This bill, however, proved to be a dead letter, because its provisions were only operative with the consent of the bishops, and they did not hesitate to use their authority against it, in the main, with the result that ritualism continued to spread. In 1890, for example, when the case of Bishop King was heard before the Archbishop, concessions were made to the ritualists which called forth the following significant comment from *The Times*:

> any country village may suddenly have a priest imposed upon it who will transform its familiar and simple form of worship into an approximation to that of Rome, and every parishioner must either submit to it or give up his Church altogether.[1]

In the famous Bennett decision of 1892 the "Romanizers" triumphed, for the accused, who had spoken of a real, actual and visible presence in the Eucharist, received a practical acquittal.

It was small wonder then that the Free Churches were alarmed as the last decade of the century dawned. It seemed to them that the future of Reformation principles rested, not with the harassed and declining Evangelical party within the Established Church, but with prompt and concerted action by themselves. To justify such a position, however, clearly demanded effective co-operation and unity of some kind among the Free Churches. Moreover, the publication of *The Secret History of the Oxford Movement*

[1] *The Times,* November 25, 1890.

by Walter Walsh, described fairly by Professor Sanday as "an indictment but an indictment with evidence produced", had alarmed many Free Churchmen who had hitherto been indifferent to the menace of ritualism, or had been inclined to minimize the serious nature of its challenge.

This alarm on the part of the Free Churches coincided with the increasing fraternal spirit which recognized the unmistakable links which, in the nature of the case, existed between the various Free Church bodies—what has already been described as "the socialistic tendency of the age"—and it needed only the stimulus of men of vision and initiative, such as the early Grindelwald conferences supplied to the Free Churches, to bring to birth the desired co-operation.

All this must be readily conceded, but it is not to say that the origin of the Free Church Council movement was anti-Anglican. There was certainly the desire to resist the spread of sacerdotalism and its intolerance, present in the minds of the early leaders of the movement, but the much needed assertion of Canon (later Bishop) Hensley Henson should be recalled, namely, that the Church of England rightly judged by its formularies, by its greatest divines, by the general tenor of its history and by the logic of its situation as a Reformed Church, is an Evangelical one.[1] Indeed, there were many people within the Anglican Church at the time of the inception of the Free Church Council movement who were as much concerned as Free Churchmen at the challenge of ritualism.

The main intention of the Free Church Council was, however, a positive and not a negative one. The leaders felt that the Free Churches were far more substantially agreed on the truths they held, and on their public policy, than the conflicting parties of the Established Church. It

[1] Hensley Henson, *The Road to Unity,* n/d, p. 48.

seemed, therefore, of paramount importance for the future of Reformed religion in England that this substantial agreement should be openly and effectively demonstrated at a time when the country's Protestant tradition seemed in imminent danger. The Free Churches came together, not merely to resist the propagation of a theory of religion which seemed to them to be in direct contravention of New Testament teaching, but to take common action on great religious and social problems, to strive together to deepen their own spiritual life, and to win England for Jesus Christ.

Two of the most prominent and influential leaders of the Free Church Council, indeed the two chief architects, Dr. Charles Berry of Wolverhampton, and the Rev. Hugh Price Hughes, both of whom played a leading part in the shaping of the policy, catechism and the constitution, entertained no idea of hostility to the Established Church. Both men presented to the world, with all their powerful eloquence, the positive idea of the Free Churches as an accredited portion of the Catholic Church, possessed of a noble and rich heritage. As Charles Berry put it, Nonconformists were not entering the New Jerusalem by a side gate but through the main entrance with colours flying.

The accusation that the Free Church Council movement was anti-Anglican in origin, cannot be sustained by an examination of the facts. That it has often been levelled is due to the unhappy circumstances of the hour of its inception, and to the thoughtless remarks made by the less enlightened people on both sides.

We shall see as we trace our story that owing to pressure of circumstance it was often forced into opposition to the Anglican Church, but we shall see too that, none the less, its real, positive, spiritual basis was never forgotten and never disappeared.

Chapter 3

ORGANIZING THE MOVEMENT

THE first Free Church Congress opened on Monday, November 7, 1892, in Manchester. Since the January meeting, Dr. Mackennal of Bowdon, the secretary of the committee charged with the arrangement of the Congress, had been extremely busy. It was fortunate that the office had been entrusted to such a man, for he was possessed of an extraordinary industry and wisdom, allied to a capacity for organization second to none. As Hugh Price Hughes said of him in later years, his selection as secretary at that stage did more than can be expressed to ensure the ultimate success of the venture. The first Congress, at any rate, owed much of the success it achieved to Mackennal's unwearied and competent planning.

The Congress had a different chairman at each session, there being no presidential office at this stage. The chairman at the inaugural meeting was Mr. Henry Lee, J.P., a prominent Manchester Congregationalist. The muster roll of the Congress showed 370 names, and 325 of these can be assigned to their respective denominations as follows: Congregationalists, 145; Wesleyan, 53; Free Methodists, 34; Primitive Methodists, 31; Baptists, 30; Presbyterians, 14; New Connexion Methodists, 12; Bible Christians, 2; Calvinistic Methodists, 2; members of the Free Church of England, 2. Membership was personal and not delegated in any way at this stage, and all members of Free, Evangelical churches were eligible on a payment of five shillings. The ticket of membership was made the ticket of admission to all sessions of the Congress except the open Public Rally.

Hugh Price Hughes and Alexander McLaren in the opening speeches, emphasized the exceptional importance of the occasion and expressed the hope that it would be but the beginning of a fellowship which would sweep away for ever all misapprehensions and points of contention between the Free Churches. The main interest of the Congress was theological. It discussed, for example, the nature of the Church, the Ministry and the Sacraments at some length and its findings were such as to indicate that no essential difference of opinion existed amongst Free Churchmen on these cardinal factors. Great attention was centred upon the practical problems of evangelism. Thomas Law of Bradford, later the organizing Secretary of the Free Church Council movement, delivered an illuminating discourse on the possibility of Nonconformist parishes and outlined in detail the success which had attended such a scheme in Bradford, where each Free Church had made itself responsible for a certain district of the city. This scheme was to become the policy and basis of later Free Church Council evangelism.

In a debate on the question of religious equality, Hugh Price Hughes in perhaps the most important address of this Congress, urged that no action must be taken which would reduce the Congress to a mere committee room of the Liberation Society, nor should the principles of that Society ever be made a *sine qua non* for membership of any Nonconformist Church. No one sympathized with the desire for Disestablishment more than Hugh Price Hughes, but he saw clearly that if the main work of the Congress should veer in such a direction, then the theological impulses which had brought the movement to birth would be by-passed, and obscured if not lost. There is little doubt that Hughes was voicing the attitude of the leaders of the Congress, and its more enlightened supporters.

On the Tuesday evening, almost three thousand people packed the famous Free Trade Hall for the only public session of the Congress. This hall, described by one present as almost consecrated to the cause of liberty, had been the scene of many famous assemblies—the Chartists, the exponents of Free Trade, Mr. Gladstone speaking on the Irish question—and it now became the stage for a large and enthusiastic gathering of Free Churchmen who were creating a precedent destined to have far-reaching effects on the religious life of England. Mr. (later Sir) R. W. Perks, M.P., presided, and the speakers were three Free Church giants—Dr. Monro Gibson, Dr. Charles Berry and Dr. John Clifford. All three were received with great enthusiasm, and all appeals for unity and co-operation were warmly applauded. John Clifford, the last speaker, wound up in his own inimitable way:

> We are making history . . . the Free Churches are on a new point in their long annals. We are entering a new chapter not only in the history of the Free Churches but in the history of religion, the history of this nation, and the history of humanity. Wake up, Oliver Cromwell, wake up the spirit of our Puritan ancestors, and once more lead us to victories for freedom and for God. . . .[1]

There were few audiences which could remain indifferent when John Clifford warmed up, and this was not one of them as their acclamation clearly showed.

The Congress appointed a committee charged with the duty of perpetuating the life of the new organization, and of taking immediate action to communicate with the denominations in the interests of Free Church co-operation. This was the only official contact that the Congress had with the denominations.

[1] *The Freeman,* November 11, 1892, for this quotation and a full account of the proceedings.

The last and most moving scene took place in Union Baptist Chapel in Oxford Road, where Dr. Alexander McLaren conducted a joint Communion Service:

> In the heart of the Free Churches, I am bold to affirm that there is one consensus in clinging to the incarnate and dying Son of God as King, Saviour, All in All. . . .

There could be no more fitting climax to the birth of a great spiritual movement than the beautiful words of Alexander McLaren.

This first Congress, inevitably, was criticized by some, but it seems to have been warmly welcomed by the majority of Free Churchmen. The major criticism centred on the fact that many of the Free Church leaders were absent, and that the number of personal members was not large. It is undeniably true that there were more Free Church leaders absent than present and that three hundred and seventy members could hardly claim to be representative of over one and a quarter million Free Churchmen and ten thousand churches. None the less, there is no doubt that the Congress was a great success and that a good deal of valuable work was done during the sessions, nor was there lacking the promise of greater things to come. Critics of this first venture, and venture it was, are inclined to forget that the movement was only in its infancy, and accordingly, many stayed away because they wished to see exactly what would happen before lending their support. Moreover, Manchester is not a central position, and the travelling facilities and conveniences were those of the nineteenth and not the twentieth century.

Some criticism was levelled at the method of membership, and hopes were expressed that the next Congress would be based on representative membership from the denominations as well as personal membership. *The Freeman*, for example, claimed that if the Baptist churches had been invited to send official representatives, the number of Baptists present would have been nearer three hundred than thirty! This particular criticism was to recur again and again, but it was not until the formation of the Federal Council in 1919 that such a method was adopted.

This first Free Church Congress was an unprecedented Nonconformist gathering, but it created a precedent which, with slight variations, was followed for many years, and it is no overstatement to say that the Congress surpassed the hopes of its most sanguine supporters. The Second Congress was not held until March 1894, and the intervening period was, for the most part, devoid of special incident. Quiet, steady but important work went on in the interests of extending the influence of the new movement.

A notable event, however, took place on February 20, 1893, when a conference of Free Churchmen was held in Birmingham under the presidency of Mr. George Cadbury, who, thoroughly alarmed at the fact that only twenty-seven per cent of the population were attending church (how staggering these figures seem to us to-day), sent out invitations to leading Nonconformist ministers and laymen in the Midlands. Almost all the invitations were accepted, and Dr. R. W. Dale, minister of Carrs Lane Congregational Chapel, was perhaps the best known minister present. The conference, after hearing the Rev. Thomas Law explain the scheme of house-to-house visitation which had worked so well in Bradford, unanimously resolved to institute a similar scheme in Birmingham, and a committee was set up to implement this at once. Dr. Dale heartily concurred and urged his own church members to give it their active and unstinted support.[1]

After this important decision had been taken, the Rev. F. Luke Wiseman, a Methodist minister in the city, pro-

[1] A. W. W. Dale, *Life of R. W. Dale of Birmingham*, 1898, p. 647.

posed that a Free Church Council be formed in Birmingham to enable the Free Churches to take concerted action on matters affecting their common interests and upon questions relating to the social, moral and religious welfare of the people. It was soon clear that this proposal would not be adopted unanimously, for it was at this point that Dr. Dale saw the parting of the ways in the choice of methods which the Christian Church should employ for the regeneration of the social life of the nation.

From the outset, Dr. Dale had regarded the Free Church Congress with the greatest suspicion, and, despite his warm, personal regard for some of its promoters like Dr. Mackennal and Charles Berry, he would take no part in the movement at all. He was silent on the matter, however, until Luke Wiseman brought matters to a head in Birmingham with his proposal. Dr. Dale felt that the time had come for him to define his attitude clearly and without possibility of any misunderstanding. He was haunted by the fear that Free Church Councils would become political and municipal caucuses. Dr. Dale regarded the Church, in its very essence, as a religious institution established solely for religious purposes. Social and political reforms, however desirable or necessary, in this view, were not specifically the concern of the Church. Once they became objects of Church activity, Dr. Dale considered that the Church might be degraded into a merely political organization and thus be diverted from the main purpose for which God had called it into being. Dale's own view of the need for reform in the life of the nation, was that first the Church should do all it possibly could in the power of the grace of Christ to renew and sanctify all its adherents, and then should send them forth as Christian men and women, but as citizens and not Church members, to leaven and transform the life of society. He felt, as others did, that the Free Church Council would not be able to stop at pronouncing a judgment on public questions but would have to interfere in local elections, municipal and political. Organized interference was the wrong method, as he saw it; the individual Christian in his daily life and witness must be the medium for the conquest of society and the ushering in of the Kingdom of God. Dr. Dale proceeded to argue from what had been accomplished in Birmingham by Nonconformists as individuals, and he doubted whether organized action would have produced half the results. Men might resent the Church's interference where they would welcome the individual Christian's effort.

Dr. Dale therefore pleaded with Mr. Cadbury's conference for delay and careful deliberation before committal to the Free Church Council movement. If the motion was carried, he declared, it would mean the parting of the ways so far as he personally was concerned. Despite his conviction and his eloquence, there were only ten dissentients when the vote was taken.

The house-to-house visitation was undertaken in May 1893, the city being divided into 161 areas with over four thousand visitors.[1] The success of the enterprise was such that it gave impetus to the formation of the Birmingham Free Church Council which was officially inaugurated on November 27, 1893. George Cadbury was the first President and remained in office until 1898, when he was succeeded by Luke Wiseman.

This is not the place to embark upon a lengthy discussion as to the merits or defects of Dr. Dale's reasoning, but the incident is important because it indicates what was the main obstacle in the path of the new movement. One must remember that Dr. Dale had a wide experience of municipal affairs and social endeavour, that he was a man of the highest possible integrity and purpose, and that his

[1] A. G. Gardiner, *Life of George Cadbury*, n/d, pp. 166–167.

reasoning has always been acceptable to certain sections of the Free Churches. Moreover, he put his case with the utmost clarity and cogency. None the less, it was quite clear that Free Church opinion in the Midlands, at any rate, was overwhelmingly against him. An official spokesman of the Free Church Council, writing at the turn of the century, pronounced the following verdict:

> History has clearly proved that the majority were right. No Council has ever been less in danger of splitting on the rock of party politics than the Birmingham Council. Its work, so nobly and generously aided by Mr. George Cadbury, has been spiritual from its first hour unto this day. The same may be said of practically all the Councils throughout the country.[1]

From February 1893 until March 1894, the impulses towards Free Church federation were gaining momentum slowly but surely. Progress at this stage did not show the spectacular advances which were to be won after 1894, but the position was by no means static. Two brief examples may be given. By November 1893 the Free Churches of Hampshire had adopted a scheme of Federation which divided the county into nine districts, each having an association of its own, and each committed to the task of promoting further federations within their districts. About the same time, the Free Churches of Northamptonshire set up a central committee to supervise the relations of the various denominations, and to protect the rights of Nonconformists throughout the county. These two examples are representative of a growing constituency of support for co-operation between the Free Churches.

There seems to be a division of opinion regarding the response made by the Free Churches to the second Con-

[1] *The Free Church Federation Movement*, a pamphlet, n/d, no indicated author, p. 20.

gress which gathered at Leeds in March 1894. Dr. G. J. Slosser[1] tells us, for example, that there were few people present, while A. G. Gardiner[2] maintains that the response was so meagre that Dr. Mackennal, up to the last moment, was uncertain whether the Congress could be held. Eye witnesses, however, tell us that the attendance was larger than at Manchester and highly representative of the Free Churches generally. It is true, however, that once again many leading Free Churchmen were conspicuous by their absence, while certain cities within easy reach of Leeds seem to have been very sparsely represented.

One must remember, however, that the movement was by no means firmly established at that point, and that there was still a good deal of apathy towards it in certain quarters. It must also be borne in mind that the great "canvassing" campaigns and tours of Charles Berry, Hugh Price Hughes and Thomas Law, which finally set the Free Churches of England alight with enthusiam for the new movement, had not yet been undertaken. The Leeds Congress was, however, a most important one for it took certain far-reaching and formative decisions.

The most important of these was upon the question of representation. Many considered that this should be based on the denominations, which should be invited to send official delegates to the congresses, thereby rendering the proceedings more authoritative. Hugh Price Hughes strenuously resisted this suggestion and, after much debate, eventually won his case. He urged that a territorial basis of representation should be employed—that is, representation of the local Free Church Councils and Federations.[3] He considered that this method would avoid sectarian

[1] G. J. Slosser, *Christian Unity—Its History and Challenge*, 1929, pp. 283f.

[2] A. G. Gardiner, *Life of George Cadbury*, n/d, p. 169.

[3] All County Federations were to be invited to send representatives, and all Councils in towns of more than 50,000 inhabitants. This was later relaxed to include smaller towns.

distinctions and differences, and would preclude compromise or the committal of the various Free Churches to any particular policy. The representatives would then meet not primarily as Baptists or Methodists as the case might be but as Evangelical Free Churchmen, thus enhancing and proclaiming their essential unity. This, while reducing the official status and consequent authority of the Congress, would make for a deeper unity, as Hugh Price Hughes saw it.

It is very easy in the light of the subsequent history of the movement to maintain that at this point a fundamental mistake was made and the power of the movement crippled at the outset. Some would say that Hugh Price Hughes adopted a hopelessly impractical and idealistic viewpoint, and unfortunately persuaded the rest to follow him. We must remember, however, that the movement in the eyes of Berry, Hughes, Mackennal, Bunting and others who had come under the potent stimulus of the Grindelwald conversations, was but the first step on the road to Christian reunion, and they therefore felt more than justified in sacrificing a measure of authority for the prospect of a deeper experience of unity which could blaze the trail for greater things.

For better or for worse, the step was taken and whatever defects the policy may have had, at least it transformed a mere debating society or "a fortuitous concourse of atoms"[1] into a type of Free Church parliament which strove to render the Nonconformist conscience articulate and to evangelize the whole of England.

Another important decision taken at Leeds was that for the future each Congress should have an official president nominated by the previous Congress. This proved to be a great improvement on the old system of appointing

[1] Words of Hugh Price Hughes in *Contemporary Review*, Vol. 71, March, 1897. "Free Church Unity—the New Movement".

different presidents for each session, and it had the additional advantage of bringing into central prominence the most revered and able of the Free Church leaders. The president appointed for the 1895 Congress, con cerning which an invitation from the Birmingham Free Church Council had been accepted, was the beloved "idol" of Wolverhampton, Dr. Charles Berry.

A further decision of notable importance was that the committee invited the Rev. Thomas Law, and the Rev. J. M. Gwynne Owen, who had initiated the Hampshire County Federation, to become joint secretaries for organizing Free Church Councils through the country. Mr. Law was appointed for the towns and Mr. Owen for the rural areas. This was to lead to a most spectacular and rapid expansion of the movement. Up to this point progress had been steady but slow, and publicity, such as it was, had been without any real drive or organization.

It is therefore clear that the movement owed much to the far-reaching decisions taken at Leeds, and that, without them, the future would have been uncertain and not a little precarious.

At this Congress, Dr. Richard Glover of Bristol assumed the mantle of Dr. Dale in an impassioned speech in which he urged that the Free Churches should keep out of all disputes between employer and employed, and should concentrate all energies on the proclamation of the Gospel. The danger to the Free Churches lay in becoming one sided. Dr. Mackennal who followed him in a typically wise and discreet contribution claimed that ministers should be abreast of such problems because they were the best possible conciliators. The main attention of the Congress was not centred upon such subjects however, for, generally speaking, the main interest was devotional and doctrinal. Certain critics have magnified out of all proportion what they have been pleased to call the "political" element in the Council movement, and would have us believe that the spirit and interest from the outset was overwhelmingly political. Such a view is a complete caricature of the real situation, and we shall see that even during the exciting days of Passive Resistance in the first decade of the twentieth century, the spiritual and devotional aspects of the movement, both on the national and the local scale, were neither lost nor minimized.

The main work of expansion was accomplished when Charles Berry, Hugh Price Hughes, and Thomas Law toured the country from end to end. Hughes and Berry who, by their unexampled toil and enthusiasm, had made themselves two of the outstanding leaders of the movement, wisely recognized that the "final sanction lay in the suffrage of the people".[1] Hugh Price Hughes laid immense stress upon the importance of the local Councils. They were the key to the success of the whole venture. The annual assemblies would be the figurehead, but in the towns and villages the Federation would do its greatest work in strengthening, inspiring and defending Free Churchmen on the scene of their daily struggles and tasks.

Hughes and Berry decided, therefore, that if the Free Church Council movement was to take root effectively, the whole of the Free Churches of the country must be stirred up to take a practical interest in it with the minimum of delay. No one could do such a work more effectively than two of the most prominent and popular figures of the day, and so this vast campaign began.

It is impossible to over-estimate the value of the work accomplished by Berry and Hughes, and in a lesser degree, Thomas Law. The main burden of speaking and preaching fell upon Berry and Hughes, and these two great orators brought to their task all the power and eloquence they could command. All areas of the country were visited. It

[1] Dorothea Price Hughes, *The Life of Hugh Price Hughes*, 1905, p. 445.

was an undertaking which made tremendous demands upon the physical, mental and nervous energies of the three pioneers. Long and weary journeys were necessitated, frequently at night, and it was not uncommon for the speakers to have three meetings in a day, quite apart from informal discussions. Hugh Price Hughes hated travelling and suffered nervously to an unaccountable degree when doing so, but we are told that no campaign was nearer to his heart than this one, nor any other cause so much part and parcel of his life. The possible federation of the Free Churches had vividly captured his imagination, and he regarded his labours for it as the chief work of his lifetime.[1] He believed with supreme faith that the new movement was destined to have a great future, and he felt that no sacrifice of personal energy and devotion was too great because the structure which he was helping to erect and anchor would be an abiding one. In the light of such a lofty conception, personal comfort and wellbeing were but small sacrifices to make. When he met Charles Berry, we are told that he at once recognized in him the constructive genius of the movement.

Charles Berry also had to suffer enormous demands upon his strength, and the drain upon it seldom ceased, but Berry delighted in herculean efforts. Well-meaning protests from his friends were smilingly brushed aside, and the insatiable demands upon his time and energy were never refused.[2] He believed that no religious movement was so full of promise as the Federation idea, provided it was wisely directed to practical ends, and he anticipated that it would give to the Free Churches a power they had never before been able to develop. Believing that competent scholarship gave much support to Free Church

[1] Dorothea Price Hughes, *op. cit.*, pp. 442–447. cf. also *Methodist Recorder*, November 20, 1902. cf. also *Methodism and England*, Maldwyn Edwards, 1943, p. 158.

[2] J. S. Drummond, *Charles A. Berry, D.D.*, 1899, pp. 122–123.

principles, he saw in the new movement an effective means by which these principles might be worked out in terms of vital, practical action, always preserving the essential spiritual foundation.

Both Charles Berry and Hugh Price Hughes, in their campaigning, began to live at such a pace that some kind of price had to be paid, sooner or later. Berry was to die in 1899, worn out at the early age of forty-seven. Even when suffering acutely from cardiac trouble, he insisted on fulfilling engagements, and on a number of occasions he suffered attacks while speaking, but he continued to ignore his doctor's orders until the inevitable happened. His life was active and triumphant to the very last, and he died whilst praying at the graveside of a friend. Hugh Price Hughes died in 1902, prematurely also, due to labours beyond his physical capacity, but he died as he would have wished—in harness—collapsing in a London street on the way back from a meeting. Both Berry and Hughes lived long enough, however, to see the movement well established, and the year which saw their great campaigns was, perhaps, the prime factor in accomplishing that end. Both men were possessed of majestic conceptions and a charity which could not be satisfied with anything but the widest religious life. Both men exhorted Free Church audiences over the length and breadth of England to overlook their divergences and meet on common ground.

Their message was so important that we must pause to examine it more closely. Both men were at the Grindelwald conferences and they considered that a *rapprochement* of the Free Churches must be the first step towards Christian reunion. They maintained that the true nature of Dissent was much more comprehensive and catholic than the narrow views which had so often prevailed. It was this large and majestic view of Nonconformity which they now disseminated among the Free Churchmen of England.

The possibility and reality of Free Churchmanship was brought home to countless thousands. Many testified that until they heard Charles Berry's vigour and lucidity in vindicating the position and rights of Free Churchmen, they had been half ashamed of their dissent. Berry, they said, made them hold their heads up and gave to them a great awareness of challenge and responsibility. Hugh Price Hughes paid his own tribute to Berry in this respect. Berry, he said, was the architect of the temple, and to him more than to any other the Free Churches owed the note of true, positive, scriptural catholicity which, he claimed, was the distinguishing characteristic of the Free Church Council movement.

The names given to Free Churchmen up to this point had been negative, such as "Dissenter" or "Nonconformist", but Berry and Hughes now placed the entire emphasis upon the positive aspect. The Free Churches must recognize themselves as a true part of the visible, Catholic Church, and they based this claim upon the New Testament conception of the Church. Wherever the presence of Christ with transforming power is found in the hearts of men, there, they claimed, is the true basis of the Church of Christ. Personal experience, therefore, was proclaimed as the touchstone of Christian Churchmanship, for conversion and sanctification were rightly to be regarded as miracles. Therefore when such evidences were present, Christ Himself was present with His blessing and sanction.

> . . . ours is the faith of the apostles and martyrs . . . we exist to affirm, illustrate and promote the New Testament doctrine of the Church. . . .

Hughes pointed out that Ignatius, the martyr bishop of Antioch, was the first to use the phrase "Catholic Church", and that his definition was the same as the Free Churchman's—"where Christ is, there is the Catholic Church".

> There is no cast-iron ecclesiastical polity in the New Testament. Christ did not abandon His Church when He established it. He remains in it . . . there is no need therefore for a rigid hierarchy. . . . He leads it to modification as the centuries require.[1]

Both Berry and Hughes, conscious that Nonconformists had not made enough of the doctrine of the Church, stressed these lofty conceptions. They taught the import of federal unity, the relation of different denominations one to another, of the impossibility that the good of one should mean the detriment of the other, of the nature of the annual Congress and the purpose of the local Councils. They claimed that such Councils, grounded in united endeavour, must issue in increased strength and effectiveness on the part of the Free Churches, and the elimination of the waste and friction which had often proved so distressing and obstructive in the past.

Hughes enjoined what was then a startling tolerance, embracing every communion from Rome to the Society of Friends. Christ Jesus, he would say, is with us *and* the rest. He stressed this because he believed that on a right understanding and practice of it the future of the Free Churches would depend, and that by a superior toleration and charity they could win the approval and support of all classes.

Hughes also urged Free Churchmen to embark upon the sweetening and purifying of public life, as well as the reclamation of the lost.

> Let us show our hatred of sin not only by preaching and praying, but by action in daily and public life. Vote and act in public life and business as if Christ is at your side. . . .

Berry did not neglect this particular aspect either:

[1] *Contemporary Review*, Vol. 71, March, 1897. "Free Church Unity: the New Movement".

. . . we claim lordship for Him in every sphere of life, not less in culture than in commerce, as much in social life as in Church praise. . . . Our nation for Christ is the motto inscribed on our banner. . . .

With such stirring and positive conceptions, Berry and Hughes went about their great task, ably supported by the organizing secretaries. Their meetings proved to be an enormous stimulus to the work of forming Councils up and down the land. There can be no doubt whatsoever that these two great Free Churchmen by the power of their thought, the cogency and eloquence of their speech, and the magnificent devotion and sincerity of their service, were the means of a great infusion of vigour and enthusiasm into Free Church life and thought. Too long the emphasis had been negative and defensive. Berry and Hughes sounded their clarion call to summon the Free Churches to play their true and full part in the religious life of England.

Dr. Elliott Binns, referring to the idea of the Catholic Church proclaimed by Berry and Hughes, pointed out that this idea would have meant nothing to Nonconformists at the beginning of the Victorian era. It was a step forward of the utmost importance, as Dr. Binns goes on to say:

This discovery of the Catholic Church by Nonconformity saved it from lapsing into barren individuality. Had it faced the twentieth century with the negative policy of the Liberation Society, disendowment and disestablishment, its fate might well have been that of the Liberal Party with which it was so closely involved politically. The vision and power of a number of great statesmen and prophets enabled it to rise above the limitations of its heritage into a clearer air.[1]

Dr. A. M. Fairbairn in 1897 could say:

It is harder perhaps to be a Nonconformist to-day than it

[1] L. E. Elliott Binns, *Religion in the Victorian Era*, 1936, pp. 486–489.

> has ever been in the history of England. The very decay of those disabilities from which our fathers suffered, has made it harder for us than for them to dissent.

In the last decade of the nineteenth century Nonconformity was in great need of a new vision and a consuming inspiration. The Free Church Council movement through the power and the leadership of men such as Charles Berry and Hugh Price Hughes, imparted that vision and infused that inspiration. That is why it is one of the great landmarks of Free Church history.

From the evangelical standpoint, the advent of the movement was timely, for there was a real danger of English Christianity becoming largely sacerdotal. Cardinal Vaughan, in welcoming such a prospect, could say:

> The present churches of the Establishment are often distinguishable with real difficulty from those belonging to the Church of Rome. The Real Presence, the sacrifice of the Mass, offered for the living and the dead, sometimes even in Latin, auricular confession, extreme unction, purgatory, prayers for the dead, devotion to Our Lady and the invocation of the saints, are doctrines taught and accepted, I am told, with a growing desire and relish for them in the Church of England.[1]

It was at such a time and amid such conditions that the Free Church Council movement came forward as the powerful champion of evangelical religion, for the Evangelical party within the Anglican Church was disheartened by reason of their disregarded protests, and often weakened by their own difficult position. Indeed, some of its members were to appear on Free Church Council platforms, pleading for Nonconformists to strain every nerve to keep the flag of Evangelicalism flying while the low church party recovered.

[1] Quoted by J. H. Shakespeare, *The Freeman*, October 5, 1894.

The third Free Church Congress met in Birmingham in March 1895 and finally established the new movement. It came together under the shadow of death, for Dr. R. W. Dale, the beloved minister of Carrs Lane Congregational Chapel, had died on March 13, exactly thirteen days before the Congress began its sessions in this famous chapel. Though Dr. Dale refused to take any part in the movement, he was loved and revered by all Free Churchmen, and one of the first items of business on the agenda was the passing of a resolution of condolence and sympathy.

The first president of Congress was Dr. Charles Berry—indeed, he was the only president of Congress, for in the following year when Hugh Price Hughes became president, the name of the assembly had been changed to the National Council of the Evangelical Free Churches. Some misunderstanding has arisen owing to this change of name, for some would claim Hughes as the first president, whereas he was, in actual fact, the second president of the movement as a whole, although the first to hold that office after the change of name.

It has been said that Dr. Berry's gifts as an orator and leader were never more conspicuously displayed than they were in his presidential address. It was in the characteristic vein of his impassioned orations during his campaigning, and it set Free Churchmen on fire. It makes stirring reading to this day with its sparkling challenge and its convincing exposition of the Free Church view. Discussing the origin of the movement, he claimed:

> The Congress was born, not made. . . . It is not so much an organization as an organism. . . . We are here not because of the scheming of men but because of the inspiration of God. . . . This is not a Nonconformist Congress whose *raison d'être* lies in a negative and critical attitude towards the Established Church. This is a Free Church Congress

> based upon our common and positive adhesion to the great verities of Evangelical history.[1]

Those words clearly indicated why the Unitarians had been excluded from the Congress. The Free Churches had been charged with a lack of breadth and brotherhood for not inviting the Unitarians to join in the movement. Dr. Berry cleared away all misunderstanding in his presidential utterance when he said:

> . . . the point on which we differ is one of such vital importance, involving the whole personality and mission of Jesus Christ, and necessarily carrying with it such difference of spiritual experience, as to render union a matter of practical impossibility.

These words settled the matter for ever, and prevented the movement from sinking into what would have been very close to humanism and philanthropy. Charles Berry felt that an uncompromising assertion of Christ's deity was needed, and he gave it. The Unitarians might be admired, but Free Churchmen could never join in Christian unity with those who questioned the fundamental truths of Christianity. The whole matter was now clarified, and, henceforth, local Councils could point to a definite ruling if and when the question of Unitarian admission arose.

At the Birmingham Congress, delegates heard with pleasure and enthusiasm of the remarkable progress of expansion. Twelve months earlier at Leeds there had been approximately 40 local Councils in existence: now there were 150, over three-quarters of which had engaged in vigorous house-to-house visitation in their areas. Increasing efforts had been made in the process of expansion to link the towns with their surrounding villages so that whole

[1] For the complete speech and account of the Congress, see *The Third National Congress of the Evangelical Free Churches*, n/d.

counties could be covered with a compact and efficient organization. By this method, those rural areas undergoing the subtle persecutions of parson and squire could be rallied and strengthened and made acutely conscious of the concern and the support of their brethren.

On the more practical side, this Congress took a number of important decisions. The Rev. Thomas Law was invited to become resident in Birmingham, with office as the Organizing Secretary, while Mr. J. Rutherford was appointed as his assistant. Mr. Rutherford had been the General Secretary of the Birmingham Sunday School Union, and had directed the Attendance at Worship Census in the city in November 1892. Hugh Price Hughes was appointed President-elect, and Mr. George Cadbury, Mr. R. W. Perks, M.P., and Mr. C. Macdonald were appointed Treasurers.

A most important step was taken when during the meetings, George Cadbury communicated with the officials concerning the financial necessities of the movement. Hugh Price Hughes was one of the men who interviewed Mr. Cadbury and laid the whole position before him, with the happy result that both George and Richard Cadbury, his brother, promised to place a considerable sum of money annually at the disposal of the movement for the purpose of covering the entire country with local Councils. This generous and willing provision secured the movement from degenerating into a mere paper organization impeded and crippled by lack of means. The debt the movement owed to the Cadburys, and to George in particular, at this critical moment in its destinies is one so great that it can never be fully assessed.

The Congress over, delegates departed with a new zeal and a new conception of what this great movement of the Free Churches might, under God, accomplish. A. G. Gardiner tells us that this Congress finally established the movement.[1] At any rate, there was now manifested a strong desire to substitute a permanent Council for an annually summoned Congress. The actual suggestion seems to have emanated from Hugh Price Hughes, and the result was that a committee was instructed to prepare a draft constitution for presentation at the next assembly.

In the meantime, the work of expansion proceeded with undiminished vigour. Berry and Hughes were again in the forefront, but it should not be forgotten that invaluable and extensive work along the same lines was accomplished by other famous Free Church leaders. Among these the names of Dr. Mackennal, Dr. John Clifford, Dr. Alexander McLaren, Dr. R. F. Horton, Dr. J. H. Jowett, the Rev. J. G. Greenhough, the Rev. F. Luke Wiseman, Dr. W. J. Townsend, Mr. Percy Bunting, Mr. R. W. Perks, M.P., and Mr. Albert Spicer, M.P., stand out. Meetings were held all over the country, and the largest buildings were packed with capacity crowds of representative and enthusiastic Free Churchmen. The labours of these outstanding campaigners and the spontaneous response they secured, clearly indicated that the days when the Free Churches might be regarded as the ugly duckling of English religious life were very definitely over.

[1] A. G. Gardiner, *Life of George Cadbury*, n/d, p. 169.

Chapter 4

MISSION TO ENGLAND

THE first National Council of the Evangelical Free Churches (the fourth Annual Congress) was held in Nottingham in March 1896 under the presidency of Hugh Price Hughes, and the most important step was the adoption of a Constitution. It was not an entirely new feature for it had been formulated along the lines of previous procedure, and it embodied very largely the habits which from year to year the Congress had inclined to pursue. In 1892 there were people who maintained that no resolutions should be passed at all, so congressional were they in character and so little responsibility did they feel entitled to assume. With the advent of increasing representation from the local Councils and Federations, however, it was felt that the delegates might at least express themselves as Free Churchmen in the voicing of certain sentiments. They could therefore claim to be, in some respects at least, the voice of the Free Churches although not of the individual denominations. In view of this general feeling, it was clear that the time had come to be a more concrete and official body for which the name "Council" would be in every way suitable, and the adoption of a Constitution would lay down a definite road to travel along.

The Constitution was adopted without dissent, and the official objects of Council policy were designated as follows:

(*a*) To facilitate fraternal intercourse and co-operation among the Evangelical Free Churches.

(*b*) To assist in the organization of local Councils.

(*c*) To encourage devotional fellowship and mutual counsel concerning the spiritual life and religious activities of the Churches.

(*d*) To advocate the New Testament doctrine of the Church, and to defend the rights of associated Churches.

(*e*) To promote the application of the law of Christ in every relation of human life.

Certain restrictions were placed upon personal membership in order to ensure that representative members could never be out-voted.

A most important step was taken in the appointment of the Rev. Thomas Law as the paid, as opposed to the Honorary, full-time Organizing Secretary. Thomas Law, who had been a minister of the Methodist Free Church for twenty-three years, resigned his pastorate, and from this time onwards the Free Church Council had the full-time service of a first-class organizer at its disposal. Testimonies to his work and his fitness for this key position came from many speakers, and the appointment was unanimous. In 1895 Thomas Law had been installed in Birmingham offices, but Free Church Council Headquarters were now established in the Memorial Hall in Farringdon Street, London, and this proved to be a most important and successful venture. Both the appointment of Thomas Law, and the removal to London, were made possible largely through the generosity of the Cadbury brothers.

There is no doubt that the National Free Church Council got off to a promising start, neither is there any doubt that it was going a long way towards satisfying the craving for a more manifest Free Church unity, and one not expressed in mere uniformity but in an inward harmony of spirit and purpose which would leave ample room for individuality, freedom and the preservation of cherished traditions. The Free Churches had come together, as never before, on the firm ground of fundamental truth and common endeavour.

By March 1896, the number of local Councils and Federations had increased from 130 to 209. More important than the actual figures was the fact that concerted action had been taken in many directions, not only in the towns but also in many rural areas. From the first, it had been recognized that to concentrate on the towns and neglect the small village causes would be a short-sighted policy. Complete County Federations had been established in Surrey, Hampshire and Northants. Elsewhere, there had been suggestions that the scheme might usefully follow the boundaries of the Parliamentary electoral divisions, but this was found to be impracticable. Finally the most feasible method was found to be that of grouping the villages of a certain area around a strong urban centre. For example, the Lincoln Free Church Council took in the villages within a radius of at least ten miles, and Boston followed suit. Thomas Law hoped to cover the whole country with a similar network of organization by means of which the strength and vigour of urban and city Free Church life would flow to the villages and provide a much needed "shot in the arm".

During these years the growth of the movement proceeded at a spectacular pace. By 1899, there were 500 Councils and Federations; by 1901 there were approximately 700 local Councils and 36 District Federations. More and more Free Churchmen in these years came to identify themselves with the new movement. Hesitancy began to ebb as the true nature of the Council became clear. There was hardly a prominent Free Church leader who was not on the Council platform, and the great majority of the rank and file were supporters and sympathizers. During these years, united missions were held in almost every main centre where the Council established itself and in many rural areas. This evangelism was surprisingly successful and in some areas assumed the appearance of revival. In 1897, Gipsy Smith became a special full-time missioner for the Council with a roving commission in all the large cities of England and Wales. There were other notable missioners who toured the country under the auspices of the Council, again with striking success. Mr. W. R. Lane, Dr. Campbell Morgan, the Rev. F. C. Spurr and the Rev. J. Tolefree Parr were the leading names, but there were many others who played a valiant part in making the Council one of the most effective instruments of evangelistic enterprise that England had seen. The campaigns and missions were carefully planned, nor was it a shallow conception of evangelism based on crudity, sensationalism and emotion. John Clifford confessed that he had always been frightened of religious hysteria and fleeting emotional excitement in religion, but at the close of his presidential visitations in 1899 he could say in all honesty that the Council evangelists had used the most enlightened methods and were appealing sincerely to conscience and intellect—in other words, methods designed to secure enduring and not transient results.

This extensive evangelism remained an integral part of Council activity and, despite what some critics believe, indisputably the central one. Over a period there was hardly a town or city in England which was not deeply stirred and challenged. It is always a mistake to try and assess the value of such activity in mere figures, for they are not an adequate category of value to employ, but even on that level one can see something of the great impact that Council evangelism made on the life of this country. Many thousands of people professed conversion and proved it by joining and remaining loyal to the Church. Indeed, many of the staunchest Free Churchmen up and down the country to-day look back to those Free Church Council missions as the time when serious Christianity began for them. Something will be said later in the chapter about the great Simultaneous Mission of 1901 which deserves a separate examination.

The local Councils engaged in many and varied kinds of work besides evangelism. A striking feature was the adoption of the Nonconformist parochial system by most of the Councils and intensive house-to-house visitation in each "parish". To stimulate this particular activity, Mr. George Cadbury gave a grant of £5 to every Council pledged to this work, the money to be used for the purchase of large-scale street maps to enable the various Free Churches to divide up the work efficiently. Educational lectures on Free Church history and principles were organized all over the country and Free Church literature was disseminated on a large scale. At Coventry, a Free Church Help Society or Benevolent Fund was set up for serious relief work among the poor; at Newport (Mon.) the Council set up a home for friendless girls; at Trumpington, near Cambridge, a joint Free Church cause was established in the place of two struggling chapels with encouraging results. In the department of social endeavour, perhaps the most remarkable result was that of the Central South London Council, who achieved in an "abandoned" district south of the Thames a minor revolution. Due to its vigilance and energy whole streets of disorderly houses and brothels were closed. In one week alone, no less than eighteen were disposed of. Tenants living on the proceeds of impurity and prostitution on their premises were proceeded against, and hardly a case was lost. Public bodies, overseers, and the police, were all encouraged to vigorous action by the discoveries and the energy of this Council.

The success of this Council was sufficient answer to those who contended that the churches should not take action in such matters but should urge their members to act as Christian citizens. The Central South London Council proved that an organized army is always and must be a better fighting force than isolated guerrillas. Many local Councils engaged in other work, much of it admittedly with a negative emphasis, such as action against Gambling, particularly Street Betting, Sunday Trading, and the extension of the Liquor Trade. Special Free Church Council Watch Committees were set up in some areas to exercise vigilance in such social concerns. For example, in November and December of 1900, a Twentieth-Century Crusade against Intemperance was launched with the avowed object of securing one million new pledges of total abstinence. The chief rally was at the Metropolitan Tabernacle, but similar enthusiastic rallies were staged in the more important provincial centres. While it is true that much of this type of work was essentially negative and directed to symptoms rather than causes, the fact remains that many of these protests were much needed to check tendencies which if unhindered would have entailed the degradation of national and social life. There is, in other words, a point where negative action of some kind is always necessary. The mistake the Council made on occasions was that of concentrating on the protest almost to the exclusion of constructive and positive remedies. One must poultice a boil, but the real trouble is usually in the blood and the real cure can only be worked there.

During these years ritualism continued to make considerable inroads upon the Established Church. In 1898, Mr. Samuel Smith[1] drew the attention of the House of

[1] See *Ritualism in the Church of England*, pamphlets. No. 2: *The Speeches of Samuel Smith, M.P. and the Rt. Hon. Sir William Harcourt, M.P., in the House of Commons*, June 16 and 21, 1898, on the Benefices Bill, p. 10.

Commons to a body called "The Order for Corporate Reunion". Mr. Smith told the House that this organization was believed to have bishops secretly consecrated who, in turn, were willing to administer reordination to Anglican clergy who were willing to submit to it. One of these secret bishops, an Anglican vicar in London, was believed to have reordained secretly several hundred Anglican clergy, and Mr. Smith considered it significant that the gentleman in question had never attempted to deny the charge. Moreover, claimed Mr. Smith, a prominent Roman Catholic publication had referred to the fact of reordination under conditions likely to be acceptable to the Roman Church. He claimed that "The Order for Corporate Reunion", as soon as a sufficient number of Anglican clergy had participated, contemplated submitting a petition to the Pope pleading for corporate reunion. Mr. Smith asked the House to examine the evidence and to take action against the members of this papal society.

Whatever truth there may have been behind these startling assertions of Mr. Smith, his statement could only have the effect of alarming Free Churchmen and of increasing their suspicion of the Anglican clergy. About this time, J. A. Kensit, a publisher of Paternoster Row, constituted himself the champion of Protestantism, and he initiated and supervised what is known to historians as "Kensit's Crusade". He and his followers were responsible for some disgraceful scenes in a number of churches suspected of Roman Catholic practices and dogma. Kensit, an Anglican himself, presented a petition to both Houses of Convocation, but failed to move the authorities who allowed the matter to drop. A new figure entered the struggle in the person of Sir William Harcourt, leader of the Liberal Party, who in a letter to *The Times*[1] supported the methods of agitation and appealed to the laity for a

[1] July 22, 1898.

resolute defence of Reformation principles. Thus encouraged, Kensit and his followers increased their efforts, while Sir William continued to pose as *fidei defensor.*[1] A further letter of his to *The Times* elicited a leader in that paper, entitled "The Crisis in the Church", which viewed the controversy as one between Protestant doctrine and a Roman revival. *The Times* cast its powerful voice and influence against the ritualists when it suggested that Lord Salisbury might throw the weight of his high office into the scale to purify the Established Protestant Church from unauthorized and unfortunate innovations. The implication of all this is that if *The Times* with its great reputation and influence felt compelled to take up such a position, then the situation within the Anglican Church was serious indeed, and the Free Churches could be readily excused for being gravely concerned. It was only natural therefore that they should seek to redouble their efforts to consolidate their own position and to resist the tide of Romanism. This is one of the reasons why the Free Church Council movement prospered and expanded so rapidly. It was the main champion of Evangelical religion in England at this time of crisis and concern, and Free Churchmen, many of whom had at first been indifferent, threw in their lot with the Council in increasing numbers.

It is no coincidence that at this time a special literature department was established at the Memorial Hall. *The Free Churchman* appeared late in 1897, edited by the Rev. F. B. Meyer, issued monthly at a cost of one penny, and described by many as a Nonconformist parish magazine. In January 1899, the *Free Church Chronicle* appeared, its object being to survey the Council movement and to

[1] Sir William resigned the leadership of the Liberal Party in December, 1898, succumbing to petty pressure from his nominal supporters. Many members wished Lord Rosebery to assume leadership. It is possible that Sir William's support of the Kensit agitation led many people to desire this change. Sir William had been inducted into the leadership by Mr. Gladstone, who died on May 19, 1898.

discuss the burning questions of the age. Many other kinds of Free Church literature were prepared and circulated by this department on a vast scale all over the country. Happily, many special gifts of money had been earmarked for this important service so that the work was in no way hindered by lack of means.

In this connexion 1899 opened with an event of supreme importance. On January 5 the Free Church Catechism was issued by the Publications Department of the National Free Church Council. The first edition of ten thousand copies was sold immediately, and within a month one hundred thousand copies had been called for. As we have seen, Charles Berry and Hugh Price Hughes had been responsible for the teaching of the comprehensive and catholic nature of modern dissent, and for the infusion of a new vision of the possibility and the reality of Nonconformist churchmanship. Both men had pleaded in 1896 for the compilation of a Free Church Catechism because both had realized the urgent necessity of defining the theological position of the Free Churches, for example in relation to the problem of Unitarianism. The necessity for this statement or catechism was dictated not only by the pressure of outside events, although that was an important factor in view of ecclesiastical tensions, but in order to express clearly the fundamental, theological unity of the English Free Churches. Hugh Price Hughes was the one who insisted on the preparation of the Catechism. It is not a bit of good, he said, proclaiming unity if there is no verbal expression of it, to which friend and foe alike can have recourse.

The work took over two years. The first draft was worked out by the Rev. Principal J. Oswald Dykes, D.D., of Westminster College, Cambridge, a Presbyterian, this initial draft being supervised and revised by a representative committee of Free Churchmen. Hugh Price Hughes was both chairman and secretary and thus convened and attended at all stages of the committee work.

The object of the Catechism was to express, not the peculiarities of any particular denomination but those fundamental and essential truths common to all the Evangelical Free Churches.[1] The representative theologians who were responsible for the final form of the Catechism were not appointed by their own denominations but by the Committee of the National Council, so that, strictly speaking, no denomination could be held responsible for it. It had, therefore, no official weight apart from the sanction of the Free Church Council. It is interesting to note that it was not prepared solely by ministers for two influential laymen worked with the ministerial revisers. The theologians who prepared it represented, indirectly or directly, the beliefs of not less than sixty million avowed Christians throughout the world. The Catechism was the response to an ever-growing appeal for an expression of Free Church doctrine which was catholic rather than denominational and which expressed theological truth in modern language. The idea was not at all to supersede ancient doctrines but to provide a restatement which avoided obsolete and ambiguous terminology. The Catechism took the form of fifty-two questions and answers which could be effectively taught on a weekly basis throughout the year.

Students of history will be aware that no such combined statement of inter-denominational belief had hitherto been attempted, much less achieved. Dr. Henry S. Lunn described the work of the Revision Committee as the first attempt since the Savoy Conference[2] by a representative

[1] See an excellent article in *The Free Church Chronicle*, June, 1899, pp. 185–186.

[2] April, 1661, between 12 bishops and 12 puritan ministers to attempt to reach agreement in regard to changes in the Prayer Book. There was no real attempt to draw up a combined statement of faith, for the Puritan point of view was set aside.

body of different Protestant communions in Great Britain, to join in one expression of their common faith.

The Catechism received notable attention from the press, and leading articles and detailed reviews appeared in many papers and periodicals. Bishop Gore described the emphasis of the Catechism on membership in the one visible Catholic Church as possibly marking an epoch in English religion.

The Catechism was adopted by many Free Church Sunday Schools, and Hugh Price Hughes optimistically looked forward to the day when Free Church children, universally, would be instructed in its tenets and would regard it as a venerable and precious heritage. The Catechism had a large sale in America and the Empire, and it appeared in many languages. The Publications Department of the National Council had the utmost difficulty in keeping pace with the demands of the trade and the public, and there is little doubt that the Catechism created widespread interest and enthusiasm. Yet to-day it is extremely hard to find a copy. It remained an academic expression of the faith and, despite its warm welcome, it did not take hold on the life of the Free Churches as it might have been expected to.

It is interesting to note that later in 1899 at the National Council Assembly held that year in Liverpool, Dr. Marshall Randles, Principal of Didsbury College, surprised the gathering by publicly dissociating himself from the Catechism. He described its eschatology as meagre and halting; its soteriology as thin and superficial; its doctrine of the Church as not essentially Free Church at all; and its doctrine of the Sacraments as one with which Dr. Gore could agree and rejoice in! Dr. Randles, moreover, strongly disapproved of the undemocratic and arbitrary manner in which it had been published. He claimed that not only had the committee issued it without reference to the Council but also the initial question of whether it was advisable to draw up a Catechism had not been considered. This condemnation of the content of the Catechism and the manner of its inception and issue did not reflect the attitude of even a minority of the Council, for Dr. Randles was the sole dissentient. It is strange that only one voice should be raised against it, and one cannot help but admire the courage and loyalty to conscience which prompted Dr. Randles to make his vigorous protest. In the light of the subsequent failure of the Catechism to establish itself in the life and thought of the Free Churches, perhaps this initial protest is the more significant.

Despite the rapid expansion of the Free Church Council and its deepening influence upon the Free Churches, there remained some who viewed it with suspicion. A good illustration of this attitude can be seen in a letter written to *The Freeman*[1] at the end of the century by one, James Jones of Griffithstown. He expressed surprise at the number of Baptists allying themselves with the Council and endorsing its propaganda which, he claimed, was aiming at the demolition of the grand old landmarks of Baptists' principles. James Jones, in a real sense, was a corporate voice, for the insular type of denominationalism was then, as it is to-day, very much alive, and there were a number of diehards and unprogressives who felt that any tendency towards Free Church unity would necessitate a certain sacrifice of the heritage for which their fathers had contended and suffered. The objection, of course, is not without validity in a number of ways, but it is open to the very serious criticism that not everything for which an ancestor suffers is, *ipso facto* and without any further consideration, a treasure of the same worth and significance in the changed circumstances of another age. One age may demand

[1] *The Baptist Times and Freeman,* Feb. 9, 1900.

separation on grounds of conscience; another may demand with even greater urgency and validity, co-operation and unity on the same grounds of conscience.

It was obvious that James Jones, because he was a corporate voice, called for a reply from an authoritative source, and the reply was not long in appearing and it came from the pen of the ubiquitous Dr. John Clifford. It was all the more authoritative because it came from one who was a staunch and convinced Baptist himself. Clifford hastened to point out that the Free Church Council was based on the principle of the absolute and unfettered autonomy of each Church and denomination which participated in the movement. It was therefore a misconception to suppose that its avowed object was to demolish the denominational treasures. A few weeks later, at the Annual Council Assembly at Sheffield in March 1900, the President, the Rev. Charles H. Kelly, a Wesleyan Methodist, endorsed Clifford's answer when he said:

> 'The Federation of the Evangelical Free Churches is in antagonism to no Church in its spiritual work. Its mission is not to interfere with the internal affairs of separate Churches, not even with the State Church as a spiritual organization.

James Jones, though he was a corporate mouthpiece, spoke only for a decided minority, for Free Churchmen in the main were solidly behind the new movement, or at any rate, in sympathy with it.

Reference has been made to the spread of ritualism within the Established Church and the consequent alarm of the Free Churches. This, inevitably, made the question of Disestablishment a live one. At the outset of the Council movement, it had been recognized that the Council should speak with caution on this controversial subject and leave the promotion of such ends with the Liberation Society.

Dr. Berry, in his Presidential address at Birmingham in 1895, made it clear that though the Council recognized the need for Disestablishment, it did not intend this subject to be connected with the main aims of the movement. In 1899 at the Liverpool Assembly, the Council, thoroughly disturbed and alarmed at the growing menace of ritualism, regarded Disestablishment as the most effective solution of the crisis. Dr. Randles claimed that the Romanists within the Anglican Church were undoing the work of the Reformation and were breaking their contract with the State. Others spoke in similar vein, and finally a resolution was carried with acclamation calling on Parliament to maintain the Protestantism of the realm but urging that the only final solution would be the dissolution of the church-state relationship.

To call for state interference on the one hand, and to condemn it on the other in terms which implied that such was the real cause of the trouble, seems to be remarkably inconsistent. Moreover, with the exception of Percy Bunting, the leaders seemed to have overlooked the fact that Disestablishment might easily have played right into the hands of the ritualists. Possibly that indeed might have happened, for, once owning no allegiance at all in name to the Protestant Sovereign as Head of the Church, the way would have been cleared for the more extreme to seek the Papal Sovereignty without exposing themselves in any way to the charge of violating their contract with the English State.

A few days after the death of Queen Victoria in January 1901, the great Free Church Council Simultaneous Mission to London began. Thorough preparations had preceded the launching of the campaign proper. A great mass of literature had poured out of the Free Church Council press, and intensive house-to-house visitation was carried out. United prayer meetings were held regularly all over

London, and many other prayer circles met in private homes. The campaign itself opened with an all-day prayer meeting. There is no doubt about the depths of spiritual feeling and sincerity behind this Free Church Council enterprise. Well though the preparations had been carried out, and splendid though the organizing and planning had been, the Council leaders recognized that the main essential, in fact *the* essential, was that God's Spirit would work through the endeavours of His servants. The Council approach, in other words, was based on sound theology—that victory over evil and the transformation of human personality is not the work of human enterprise, though God accepts and uses that, but of the redemptive power of God in action.

The official opening of the Mission was at Guildhall on January 28, with Dr. Joseph Parker officiating. This was the first Free Church service ever to be held in that historic building, and the event was signalized by the presence of the Lord Mayor and the Sheriffs. Many prominent Free Church leaders were in charge of the Mission in various parts of London. Gipsy Smith was at the Metropolitan Tabernacle; the Rev. John McNeill at the City Temple; the Rev. F. B. Meyer at Exeter Hall; Dr. John Clifford at Bishopsgate Chapel; the Rev. C. Silvester Horne at Union Chapel in Islington; Hugh Price Hughes at Streatham Wesleyan Chapel; Dr. P. T. Forsyth at Highgate Presbyterian Church; Dr. Monro Gibson at Kensington Town Hall; the Rev. J. Tolefree Parr at Ealing; the Rev. J. D. Jones at Woodford; and many other well-known preachers took part, including Dr. Campbell Morgan and the Rev. J. H. Jowett. At Clerkenwell, well-to-do Wesleyan business men, who were old Leysians, toured the streets with sandwich boards advertising the Mission.

F. B. Meyer estimated that the missioners reached

200,000 people every day, and as the crowds were constantly changing, an enormous number of people must have come within the reach of the Mission quite apart from the many thousands who were contacted by visitation, tracts and open-air work. The Rev. Charles Williams, in his column in the *Baptist Times*, put the daily attendance at the same figure, and claimed that 100,000 disciples were won for the Christian Faith.

The impression which the Mission made was greatly intensified by the effect on the public of the death of Queen Victoria. Observers maintained that a sense of God and eternity was in the air, and that the sorrow felt by the man in the street at what was akin to a personal loss, made many people the more ready to listen and respond to the Gospel than they might otherwise have been.

It is almost impossible to estimate with any degree of accuracy what was the total effect upon London. One very definite result was that a much better understanding between ministers and missioners than had hitherto existed was reached. Another definite result was recorded in the effect upon Free Church preaching. Ministers began to realize that it was not enough to preach about the Gospel—what was needed most of all was a clear and enthusiastic witness to its power and reality. This was a lesson which Free Church ministers in 1901 needed to re-learn. A similar effect was perhaps the greatest result of the Billy Graham Mission and the Christian Commando campaigns in our own day. A deepened devotion within the Free Churches was also a definite result of the 1901 endeavours, nor can it be denied that the Kingdom of God was considerably extended, although it should be borne in mind that F. B. Meyer maintained that the converts were won largely from the ranks of Sunday School members and those on the fringe of the Church. The effect on the general non-Churchgoing public does not seem to have been large, although a certain number of converts were won from that quarter.

It was, of course, only to be expected that one single effort would not sweep in large numbers of those who were completely indifferent to the claims of Christianity, and it was a healthy sign that the Free Churches recognized this fact in their determination to make further plans and continue vigorous evangelism. They did not allow the steam which had been generated to vanish away silently into thin air.

The Simultaneous Mission in the Provinces opened soon after the close of the London campaign, that is, about the middle of February 1901. Any comprehensive account of this great undertaking is out of the question, but a selection of the more outstanding features will be of interest and relevance to our story.

At Birmingham the chief missioners were Gipsy Smith and Dr. John Clifford. Extensive preparations had been made and visitation was caried out in one hundred and fifty Free Church parishes. When the meetings commenced, the testimony of the police force was that never before had they contended with such crowds, not even at the gatherings held for Joseph Chamberlain. Birmingham Town Hall was filled every night, and overflow meetings had to be held in Carrs Lane Chapel and the Central Hall. On one Sunday evening, when the mission service was scheduled to begin at 7 p.m., the building was packed at 5.30 p.m., and over five thousand people were still clamouring for admission! When Gipsy Smith arrived, he found himself unable to get to the building at all, and finally only managed to gain admittance with the stalwart assistance of four burly policemen!

Nowhere were preparations more thorough than at Liverpool, where the city was divided into 29 sub-districts, in each of which intensive house-to-house visitation took place. On the first evening of the mission over 30,000 attended and thousands had to be turned away. Here the missioners were the Rev. J. Tolefree Parr, Dr. G. S. Barrett, and the Rev. Alexander Connell, and all the meetings seem to have been impressive and acceptable. The *Liverpool Daily Post*, a paper whose opinion, then as now, is to be valued, commented in the following generous terms:

> There was an absence of crude sensationalism . . . an endeavour to reach the highest instincts of man, to touch into life his supreme hopes . . . quiet, thoughtful searching at one time grappling with men's sins, at another unveiling the glory of the Christian life and service. . . .[1]

Manchester, too, had an inspiring time. The most complete house-to-house visitation the city had ever known was undertaken, and during the mission more than 660 meetings were held. Unfortunately, Hugh Price Hughes the chief missioner was suddenly taken ill, but John Clifford, Alexander McLaren and J. H. Jowett willingly filled the breach. Reports showed that it was the biggest, most impressive and most successful piece of evangelistic enterprise ever carried out in the Manchester area.

The *Newcastle-on-Tyne Leader*, describing the mission in that city, paid a signal tribute to the Free Churches:

> There is in the progress of the Simultaneous Mission in Newcastle, evidence of a wonderfully concerted energy on the part of the Free Churches. A very conspicuous feature of the proceedings is the manner in which the different denominations have successfully effaced themselves.

Another significant comment came from Mr. William Angus, J.P., of Westgate Road Baptist Church, Newcastle:

> There has been in my experience no religious movement since the time of Moody and Sankey to compare with it,

[1] Quoted in *Free Church Year Book 1901*, p. 226.

and in some respects this strikes me as more impressive.[1]

The large cities and towns, however, were not the only scenes of evangelism and spiritual awakening. Some of the most striking results were witnessed in the small villages of Northumberland and Durham. In one tiny village alone, one hundred and seventeen inquirers came forward at the end of one service.

Many other stirring accounts could be given, but enough has been shown to establish the fact that spiritual results of the most gratifying nature attended the great mission in the provinces, both in the deepening of Christian convictions and the transformation of many who had never before encountered the challenge and power of the Christian gospel. Packed congregations in all places where the Free Church Council promoted this great mission, testified to the fact that God had reserved a rich blessing for this vast, united spiritual enterprise.

The *Methodist Times*, commenting on the mission, claimed that nothing would have been more entirely after John Wesley's heart or more completely in accord with the best traditions of Methodism. The writer pointed out that:

> one fatal effect of Moody and Sankey was that the organization was represented everywhere by a scratch committee called together for the mere purpose of carrying out the enterprise and dissolving when Moody had gone, but with the Simultaneous Mission, there are Free Church Councils —a guarantee of permanence which could not be given to casual missions.

The mission proved that there was no serious prejudice against Christianity on the part of the general public. It proved also that the Free Churches together could develop a concentration of energy from their hitherto latent re-

[1] Both quotations, see *Free Church Year Book 1901*, pp. 227f.

sources, which they could never hope to produce separately. Again, the mission refuted in the most effective way possible those who maintained that the Free Church Council was a political and social organization. A body which could successfully and harmoniously organize and execute the most intensive and concentrated evangelism that England had ever seen, and a body whose work had so manifestly been used of God, could hardly be classified as a political caucus. In this united evangelism, the Free Church Council had shown its true colours to the world, and it was recognized by the Council as a whole that this Simultaneous Mission was but a beginning in the arduous battle for the conversion of England. The mission had the most happy effect upon the Council. No longer was it a committee of Church leaders. Both the leaders and the rank and file had now been through a great campaign together, and had emerged as seasoned troops with heightened morale and a new sense of purpose. In their councils they had often talked about the Christian gospel. In 1901 they knew as perhaps never before that it could still work mightily.

In 1901, at the Annual Assembly of the Free Church Council held at Cardiff, a unanimous opinion was expressed upon the South African War. The previous year there had been a tacit understanding not to discuss the subject. Hostilities in South Africa had broken out in October 1899, and some Free Churchmen were in favour of stopping a war which seemed to them to be both unjust and unnecessary. The 1901 resolution is of some importance, but is far too long to reproduce in full.[1] The long and ponderous sentences in which it is couched seem very strange to us in an age which lives at a far greater pace than the Edwardian. Suffice it to say that the wording was carefully chosen, no opinion being expressed on the blame-

[1] *Free Church Year Book 1901*, p. 22.

worthiness of one side or the other. It was a resolution, admittedly, to which almost anyone could subscribe except those who openly preached hate towards the Dutch, and yet, in its way, it was an admirable and sober comment on the awful tragedy of two Christian nations resorting to the tragic arbitration of the sword.

In July 1901, some four months after the resolution was passed, a conference of Free Church ministers came together at the Memorial Hall, largely through the initiative of John Clifford and F. B. Meyer, to endeavour to find some reasonable basis of peace in connexion with the South African War. John Clifford put forward his famous six points,[1] but Dr. R. F. Horton urged that the meeting should commit itself only to a statement in general terms condemning vindictiveness and pleading for an honourable settlement. Dr. Horton[2] urged this course because he felt that Free Churchmen would never agree upon precise terms and yet he felt the urgent need for some clear statement of the Free Church point of view. If this sounds strange to us over half a century later we must beware of imposing our conditions upon that age. The Free Church voice counted for much in those days and caused many a Cabinet to tremble! This meeting set up a committee which produced a manifesto which was found acceptable and adopted. Such notable Free Churchmen as John Clifford, R. F. Horton, F. B. Meyer, W. B. Selbie, C. Silvester Horne and J. H. Shakespeare had helped to formulate the interesting contents of this manifesto. The document expressed the deep concern of the Free Churches at the long war and the bitter suffering involved, and then proceeded to indicate the lines along which an honourable

[1] Sir James Marchant, *Life of John Clifford*, 1924, pp. 145–153.

[2] Dr. Horton was attacked as a pro-Boer, and it is true that some people left his Church because of this accusation. He was never a pacifist, but he was much disturbed by "the hard grab for gold and land and glitter". R. F. Horton, *Autobiography*, 1917, pp. 201–203.

peace might best be secured. It embodied with some modification and addition the six points which John Clifford had originally suggested. It called for a generous amnesty as far-reaching as possible; compensation for the destruction of homes and property; the autonomy and self-government of the South African states under the British flag with a view to an ultimate Federation; adequate safeguards against future military strife; and urged that nothing be done which might retard the future amity and unity of the South African peoples. The manifesto called on the British people to confirm these proposals with constitutional authority, and to publish them to the Boer peoples. Those who had drafted the manifesto felt that the speedy termination of the war could best be secured by an open declaration of a pacific purpose, and an appeal was made for all Free Church ministers to sign the document as soon as possible.

The manifesto, not unnaturally, aroused widespread interest both in religious and political circles, and the Press gave a good deal of attention to it. Dr. Clifford came in for some criticism for changing his views on the war—he had previously deplored it and now seemed to be favouring British annexation—but he skilfully defended himself in the columns of the *Daily News*. Many Free Churchmen disagreed with the manifesto; for example, the Rev. Thomas Spurgeon, son of the great C. H. Spurgeon, and the Rev. J. Hirst Hollowell, who opposed Clifford on the ground that all war was unjust and annexation unlawful. This, however, was an over-simplification of the problem and was divorced from the practicable possibilities of the situation. Clifford and his supporters realized that there was not the remotest chance of peace being based on the independence of the Boers, and they set out therefore to indicate the best solution of the problem from that presupposition. They knew that no one could deny the flagrant injustices of the Transvaal administration, nor did they believe that anyone could seriously doubt that the Boers would receive liberty, justice and practical autonomy under the British flag. The solution, therefore, as they saw it, was not a clear-cut question of what was right or wrong in the abstract, and they accordingly made their appeal to reason and the practical possibilities of the situation.

During these years, and subsequent ones, most Nonconformists were Liberals, and frequently, in connexion with social and political problems, the voice of Nonconformity was similar to the cry of Liberal politics. On that account, some have supposed that there was an organic connexion between the Liberal Party and the Council movement, and that the latter could justly be described as a committee room of the political party. There is not a vestige of truth in such a supposition. Such activity of the Council which had any association with social and political problems, issued not from a puppet of a party political caucus but from a body who, because their consuming interest lay in the religious realm, deemed it necessary that a moral and spiritual—a Christian—influence should be brought to bear with the greatest possible force on specific problems or evils which necessitated such a judgment or influence. In other words, the Free Church Council believed in translating Christian theory into vital practice even at the cost of stirring up opposition and misunderstanding—even at the cost of having its motives impugned by fellow Christians, and sometimes by fellow Nonconformists.

By 1901, the movement had crystallized in method and organization and had displayed its chief characteristics and *raison d'être*. It was by then firmly established by reason of a remarkable expansion and it had already been the means of promoting a real sense of unity among the Free

Churches. In a decade in which ritualism was making considerable inroads within the Established Church, the Free Church Council represented the main centre of, and the chief rallying point for, Evangelicalism. The Council had been the means of promoting also in these years some of the most intensive, determined and effective evangelism in the history of Christianity in the British Isles. The Council was therefore an expression of real spiritual unity and purpose, and at any rate, by the end of 1901, it had not been false to the impulses which had brought it to birth.

The year 1902 ushered in a period of controversy and tumult in which the Council felt bound to take action. Whether in this exciting and troublesome time of the education controversy and the Passive Resistance movement, the Council lost its spiritual vision, we must now turn to consider.

Chapter 5

A CONSCIENCE ON EDUCATION

WHEN the National Council met in Bradford in March 1902, the Education Bill had not yet been introduced into Parliament but the King's speech had indicated that educational reforms were on the way, so that the shadow of Education hung over the assembly. The president, Dr. W. J. Townsend of the Methodist New Connexion, voiced the sentiments of the delegates when he asserted the principle that every school assisted by public funds should be adequately controlled by the public. The assembly favoured the old School Board system and showed that they would deprecate any attempt to destroy them or to curtail their power.

The long-awaited Bill was introduced into Parliament on March 24, 1902,[1] some two weeks after the Council had dispersed. The prime cause of the Bill was the financial plight of the Voluntary or non-Provided schools, which could not approach the standard of the Board Schools and which were declining seriously through lack of resources. Again, in view of the increasing development of local government through county and district councils, strong objections were felt by some to the existence of *ad hoc* bodies, particularly the School Boards with their independent power to call on rate aid. It was considered by those who framed the Bill that to abolish the Boards and transfer the administration of education to the municipal and other

[1] There followed a Special Bill for London in 1903 along the same lines but adapted to the special circumstances of the London area.

local authorities would tend to cut out extravagance and ensure a balanced judgment from people accustomed to the control of local concerns. The new Bill therefore proposed a new educational authority—the County Council in counties, and the Borough Council in county boroughs, each working through a committee composed of people well acquainted with educational needs. These committees were to control all secular instruction in elementary schools, whether voluntary or rate erected. They were to control the Voluntary Schools by appointing one-third of the Managers, by inspection, by finance and other means. Voluntary Schools were to receive the full cost of their maintenance but were to be responsible for their own repairs and alterations. The famous Cowper-Temple clause, prohibiting denominational teaching in provided schools, was retained. The Bill also made improvements in the realm of Secondary Education, and attempted to co-ordinate elementary, technical and secondary branches. There is no question that the Bill contained much that was admirable and represented in its way an educational advance.

The Bill, however, most certainly offended the Free Churches. The Free Church Council strongly condemned the Bill on the grounds that it proposed to maintain Voluntary Schools out of the rates without real public control; and because it proposed no specific, representative Education authority, embracing popular control, in place of the old School Boards. Free Churchmen were quick to appreciate that under its provisions, public money would actually be spent on the teaching of dogmas and doctrines of a sectarian nature, and that in many places teachers, and candidates for certain training colleges, would be subject to ecclesiastical tests.

Nonconformity found itself unable to resist the challenge. On April 15 its voice was heard in earnest when over eleven hundred delegates, representing over eight hundred Free Church Councils, gathered to assist principle and resist tyranny, as Mr. Percy Bunting aptly put it. This gathering condemned the Bill on the grounds that it would reverse English educational policy without the warrant of the people, as Parliament had received no mandate at the last election to undertake such a measure; and because Nonconformists would be compelled to pay rates and taxes to schools whose religious teaching was repugnant to their conscience. Hugh Price Hughes in an impassioned speech, ominous in its tone, warned the Government that:

> the authority of the British Parliament ends when it violates the sanctity of our consciences.

The Rev. R. J. Campbell went even further. He pointed out that the Free Church Council represented more than half of the religious forces of the country, and that a united Nonconformity was strong enough to turn out any government. This gathering received some considerable notice in the Press. The *Daily News* said:

> The meeting revealed British Nonconformists full of fire and fight. . . .

while *The Times* with eloquent reserve described the gathering as:

> characterized by the greatest unanimity and enthusiasm.[1]

This great protest was followed by smaller ones all over the country—indeed most cities, towns and villages held at least one meeting of protest. The National Council quickly went to work. Thousands of leaflets were printed and distributed all over the country, and letters were sent to all Free Church ministers appealing for the churches to put forth every effort to defeat the proposals. A Free Church deputation waited on Sir Henry Campbell

[1] For an excellent account of this meeting, see *Free Church Chronicle*, May, 1902, pp. 118–122; also *Free Church Year Book 1903*, p. 189.

Bannerman, leader of the Liberal Party, to plead for Liberal opposition to the Bill. Opposition and indignation increased steadily throughout the land and culminated in the famous deputation which waited upon Mr. Balfour at the House of Commons on June 12, 1902. This was the strongest Free Church deputation which had ever waited on a Conservative minister, and before meeting him, a prayer meeting was held in one of the rooms of the House. Some people would have us believe that the attitude of the Free Church Council to the Education Bill was largely due to the more pugnacious and bigoted elements within it. That this was decidedly not the case can be seen by recalling some of the famous, fair-minded and respected men who made up this historic deputation; for example, Dr. P. T. Forsyth, Dr. R. F. Horton, Dr. A. M. Fairbairn, Dr. Mackennal, Dr. Monro Gibson, Dr. Guinness Rogers, Dr. Rendel Harris, Professor A. S. Peake, the Rev. J. H. Shakespeare, the Rev. C. Silvester Horne, David Lloyd George, M.P., and many others, including, of course, the irrepressible John Clifford. At least one famous woman was present, Mrs. George Cadbury.

The deputation address, which was read to Mr. Balfour[1] by Principal Fairbairn of Oxford, was a memorable document. It possessed a clarity, cogency and determination which no doubt contributed to Mr. Balfour's obvious discomfiture while it was being read. The general argument stressed the fact that the Free Churches represented one-half of the religious forces of the country, and that the education proposals would entrust to the other half functions and duties affecting the people as a whole, functions which belonged emphatically to the State, whose concern was with all Englishmen and not merely a certain section. Moreover, the Bill would shut out of the teaching profession many of sincere conscience by increasing the range

[1] *Free Church Year Book 1903*, pp. 191–193.

and disqualifying force of ecclesiastical tests. The address went on to condemn the Bill on constitutional grounds. In the 1900 Election, the government outlined no educational proposals; had it done so, it would not have received the votes of many people who helped it to power. Therefore, justice and freedom demanded that the measure be referred to the will of the electorate. The address closed with words which contained a scarcely veiled threat:

> To carry legislation is one thing: but to prevent the disasters it would entail is quite another. We love education as we love religion . . . we have worked and suffered for both . . . but to the legislation which creates an ecclesiastical monopoly in the schools of the people, *we will not submit.*

At the close of the address, Dr. Fairbairn said plainly that he regretted that Mr. Balfour had not shown fuller and more practical acquaintance with the working of the educational system. A copy of the address was sent to every member of both Houses.

There was no doubt that the great majority of Free Churchmen were strongly opposed to the Bill, although numbers of Wesleyans of Conservative tendencies supported it because their own Voluntary Schools stood to benefit by the new legislation. For example, in 1903, there were three distinct divisions within Methodism in relation to the Education Act. A minority supported Passive Resistance; some, mainly Tory, following the lead of W. L. Watkinson, strongly condemned Passive Resistance; others, friendly to Liberalism, protested against the Bill but not to the extent of becoming Passive Resisters. Eventually the 1903 Methodist Conference accepted a resolution expressing no opinion on Passive Resistance but sympathy with those who felt that they must make such a protest, and asking the Government to pay heed to the conscientious convictions of so many Englishmen.

Free Church counter activity continued unabated in an

endeavour to stir up such a body of public opinion as would ensure the withdrawal of the Bill. For the second time, all members of both Houses were circularized, and in addition all municipal electors received leaflets urging them to vote only for candidates who would press for the Bill's removal. There was no doubt at all that feeling was running high in Free Church circles, and in August 1902 the Leeds Free Church Council decided by a majority of eighty to one, to form a League against the payment of the Education rate should the Bill become law.

On August 12, 1902, the first of Dr. Clifford's now famous letters to the Press regarding Education appeared. No account of this stage of the controversy would be complete without reference to these important and notable protests. They demonstrated a ready marshalling of facts and apt quotation, and his replies to the Archbishop of Canterbury, Lord Cecil and Canon Henson surprised many of his opponents by their lucidity and cogency. There is little doubt that these letters stimulated Free Church resistance to a remarkable degree and, moreover, powerfully impressed the general public. Clifford exposed the Bill to a withering criticism which demonstrated his complete acquaintance with and mastery of its contents. Dr. Joseph Parker commented:

> Letters like Dr. Clifford's are not casually shaken out of a man's coat sleeve. They are full of knowledge, argument and experience, and must by sheer cogency of reasoning have carried conviction to all open minds. . . . Some of us may perhaps sit on the fence and watch how the fight is going but the intrepid Clifford is instantly in the midst of the battle, and there is no mistaking the length and weight of his desperate sword. . . . I could not say less about my friend's noble letters without feeling that I was guilty of criminal silence. [1]

[1] For this and Mr. Balfour's words, C. T. Bateman, *John Clifford*, n/d, pp. 262 and 264.

Mr. Balfour did Clifford the honour of replying to him in a pamphlet:

> It can hardly be counted a waste of time to devote a few pages to the consideration of so important a masterpiece.

This reference was to Clifford's pamphlet, *The Fight against the Education Bill*, which Mr. Balfour admitted had circulated in hundreds of thousands, and had supplied the text of innumerable sermons and addresses.

Dr. Robertson Nicoll, the editor of *The British Weekly*, played a notable part in the controversy. He reinforced and defended Free Church resistance to the Bill with his powerful and brilliant pen in a whole series of leading articles in his own paper, along with signed contributions to the daily papers, particularly the *Daily Mail*.

The example set by the Leeds Free Church Council was quickly followed in other parts of the country, notably at Weymouth and Swindon. Demonstrations against the Bill increased with alarming speed, and at Woodhouse Moor in Yorkshire in September over 100,000 people took part. Indeed, Yorkshire, and in particular the West Riding, was the scene of many mass meetings. Very determined and bitter opposition developed in this area, and Charles Trevelyan, M.P., and Walter Runciman, M.P., toured the area for a fortnight's campaign under the auspices of the Free Church Council.

In Leeds and Cardiff, the results of municipal bye-elections showed that popular feeling was running strongly against the Bill, while at Leicester over ten thousand people packed the Market Place in a mass demonstration of protest. Public feeling may also be gauged from the results of Parliamentary bye-elections which took place while the Bill was proceeding through its parliamentary battles. Most of these elections can be said to have been fought largely on the Education issue. At Bury, a Liberal turned a Tory majority of 849 into a Liberal majority of 414. At Leeds, in July, a Tory majority of 2,517 was turned into a Liberal victory to the tune of 758. At Sevenoaks, in a Tory stronghold, the majority was reduced from 4,812 to 891. In November the Liberal vote for Cleveland was increased, while in the Orkney and Shetland Islands the Liberals took the seat from the Unionists by a majority of over 2,600. This run of success however did not deter the Government but only served to spur them on to force the measure through, as it appeared that there would not be another opportunity of passing it.

In November 1902 there was a remarkable rally at the Alexandra Palace when some fifteen thousand people were inside and another four thousand on the terrace. The feature of the rally was the extraordinary reception accorded to John Clifford. Public men present claimed that such a reception had not been paralleled since the retirement of Mr. Gladstone. Both Sir Henry Campbell Bannerman and Mr. Asquith, who were present, received great applause, but the greeting for John Clifford was nothing short of tumultuous.

As we have seen, more and more Free Churchmen were deciding that they must refuse to pay the Education rate if the Bill became law. Some felt that the Free Church Council should take some action about this, but others had serious qualms. Accordingly local Councils were circularized and asked for their views upon the matter. A great majority declared in favour of Passive Resistance. In December, therefore, the National Committee assembled in Birmingham to discuss the problem. The deliberations of this group revealed that a number of members, although not a majority, were opposed to any such counter measure. It was clear that the Free Church Council, as such, could not officially organize and sponsor a Passive Resistance movement. Accordingly a Special Passive Resistance

Committee was set up comprising those who were determined to organize opposition. It should be emphasized that this was not a sub-committee of the Council in any way but operated on its own entirely. None the less, it should be clearly understood that the Council was unanimous in its opposition to the Bill, and was only divided in relation to the manner and method by which that opposition should be demonstrated. The main leaders of the Resistance Committee were John Clifford, the Rev. R. J. Campbell, the Rev. C. Silvester Horne, the Rev. J. H. Shakespeare and the Rev. Thomas Law.

The National Council thus refused to commit itself to Passive Resistance, but it very definitely indicated that it would oppose the Bill in other ways, such as in its operational difficulties when it became law, and by capturing Borough and County committees, so that the Act should be administered as efficiently, and with the minimum injury to National Education and the Free Churches, as possible.

The formation of the National Passive Resistance Committee was a solution of a very difficult problem, for everyone felt that the unity and solidarity of the National Council should be preserved at all costs. It was obvious from the cleavage of opinion on the General Committee that the Council could not become the executive power behind a No-Rate movement. Insuperable difficulties were in the way, and notable and respected leaders such as Dr. Guinness Rogers, Dr. Scott Lidgett and Dr. Mackennal considered that the rate should be paid. Mackennal, for one, did not like the self-consciousness that the movement for resistance would evoke, but he declared that it was harder for him to stand aside from men with whom he had everything in common, than it would be to let the bailiff into his house to distrain upon his goods. As there could be no uniform policy, it was far wiser to let Clifford and his followers lead the way alone. The fact that the headquarters of the Resistance Committee were set up in the Memorial Hall has misled some people into thinking that the resistance was sponsored by the Council. Let it be repeated again that such was not the case and that there was no official connexion between the two bodies.

There were other Free Churchmen who agreed with the Passive Resistance protest but questioned the organizing of conscience. They felt that such resistance could be safely left to the individual conscience without any organization being used to coax or to support him. Of such persuasion was Dr. Fairbairn of Oxford who, whilst approving of Passive Resistance, could not participate for the simple reason that he did not pay rates.

The Education Bill received its third reading in the Commons on December 3, 1902, and was passed to the Upper House. It had been forced through the Commons by a process of closure of compartments—a measure only adopted previously by Mr. Gladstone over the Irish Home Rule Bill after he had been returned with an actual mandate for it. Some important clauses were actually forced through without discussion and this in relation to a measure which concerned the life of the nation to a vital degree. In the Lords, the Bill passed with little difficulty despite the protests of the Bishop of Hereford, Dr. Percival, who described it as embodying the policy of grab. The Bill received the Royal Assent on December 18, 1902 and became the law of the realm. The gauntlet had been thrown down and Free Churchmen prepared to accept the challenge.

The Act did not come into force until March 26, 1903, but by the turn of the year local Free Church Councils were forming Vigilance Committees to watch over the Trust Deeds of schools and the constitution of local Education Committees. The Legal Committee at Council

Headquarters were making careful preparations to deal with problems connected with the working of the Act, and everything pointed to the fact that there would be persistent opposition from Free Churchmen, far and wide.

Nor were signs wanting that Free Churchmen would not be alone in the struggle. Passive Resistance Leagues and Citizens' Leagues were springing up all over the country even as early as January 1903. John Clifford, Silvester Horne and the Rev. R. J. Campbell travelled thousands of miles visiting the various opposition groups and promoting their growth and influence. Ultimately the various groups were brought into one National League in 1909, but at this stage, various bodies seem to have existed, some of them representing citizens who were not Free Churchmen but who, nevertheless, would have none of the new Act.

One of the first refusals to pay the Education rate seems to have been at Oxford about the end of April when the Free Churchmen concerned refused the sectarian part of the rate, and sent their cheque to cover the ordinary rate and the old School Board rate. The collectors refused to accept the latter and the law took its course. The offending Free Churchmen were summoned before the magistrate and subsequently suffered distraint upon their goods. Oxford Free Churchmen put out an explanatory manifesto under the leadership of Principal Fairbairn of Mansfield College. This and similar events only served to stimulate the growth of resistance. A Passive Resistance Union was formed in connexion with the Presbyterian Church of England, and the Primitive Methodists came down solidly on the side of resistance, but among the Wesleyans the divisions of opinion already referred to, continued to appear. The attitude of the Wesleyan Conference may be summed up in the following passage from *The Methodist Weekly* of January 8, 1903:

So long as Anglican and Roman Catholic day schools flourish under this Act, let Wesleyan schools flourish likewise. When we can reverse the present reactionary legislation, let us do so and cheerfully merge our Wesleyan schools, but not before then.[1]

It seems that as late as May 1903, Mr. Balfour was unaware of the extent of the organized resistance. He is reported to have said that he knew little or nothing about the Committee for Passive Resistance, but he trusted that no person of sense would embark upon an undertaking equally at variance with sound logic, sound morality and sound constitutional law. There is little doubt that Mr. Balfour seriously underestimated the mettle of Free Churchmen, in expecting opposition to the Act to spend itself and die away.

On May 23 amazing scenes were witnessed when well over a hundred thousand Nonconformists, Educationists and Trade Unionists united in a huge demonstration in Hyde Park. Public interest was keen and traffic was almost at a standstill, although the King managed to drive through and so witnessed a scene he was never to forget. Processions with bands playing and with banners and streamers flying added colour to the scene. Enumerators estimated the total attendance to be in the region of 140,000. It was the largest and most enthusiastic demonstration held in the Park for over a score of years, according to the sober judgment of *The Times*. Clifford's fighting speech was cheered to the echo, and when a resolution condemning the Education Bill was put simultaneously at twelve platforms, the dense mass of humanity sprang to life. A great wave of enthusiasm swept through the Park, the cheers were thunderous and the air was alive with fluttering handkerchiefs.

[1] *Methodist Weekly*, January 8, 1903. cf. Minutes of Uniting Conference, 1932, pp. 31, 33.

Passive Resistance continued to spread appreciably, and prominent Free Churchmen indicated their readiness to go to prison rather than pay the rate. T. R. Glover, the famous Cambridge scholar, the Rev. Charles Brown, minister of Ferme Park Baptist Church, and Dr. R. F. Horton were but a few of those who rallied to the battle. Even in strong Unionist centres like Birmingham and Liverpool the movement made appreciable progress. The Countess of Huntingdon's Connexion at its Annual Conference unanimously passed a resolution approving Passive Resistance.

It was apparent to the unbiased observer that Passive Resistance could not be explained away by saying that it was merely due to irresponsible and anti-nomian tendencies within the Free Churches, although many of its opponents used unguarded epithets in their comments on the protest. For example, the speaker at the Annual Congress of the General Association of Church School Managers and Teachers referred to Passive Resistance as "Passive Humbug" and "a campaign of lies", while Mr. Winston Churchill is said to have described it on one occasion as "pantomimic martyrdom". Harsh words on both sides were inevitable in the heat and tension of that exciting age, but there was no doubt at all that some of the most cultured, respected and able citizens of England discovered that, for conscience sake, they must range themselves unreservedly at the side of John Clifford, who by now was probably the best-known man in England.

Moreover, many Free Churchmen who at first had been opposed to the extreme course, were beginning to feel that they could no longer stand aside when examples of the needless brutality and insolence of the law became apparent. At Wirksworth in Derbyshire, for example, goods worth many pounds were sold to settle a dispute involving only a few paltry shillings, and there were many other instances of excessive and vindictive distraint which only served to exacerbate feeling, stiffen opposition, and to decide many waverers to throw in their lot with the resisters—the very result which the authorities who were responsible for such treatment wished to avoid.

On July 11, another mighty demonstration was held in the Albert Hall. This was in some ways more remarkable than the Hyde Park episode, for the religious question was more prominent than the political. The hall was packed with over fifteen thousand people and many thousands were disappointed and turned away. Many people arrived in high brakes adorned with pictures of John Clifford, and bearing huge posters such as "For Conscience Sake" and "No Say—No Pay!" When Clifford was called upon to address the gathering, an amazing scene ensued. The audience rose to its feet as one man, and the air was alive with fluttering handkerchiefs and waving programmes. Cheer after cheer was raised, and several times Clifford tried to speak, but was prevented by the cheers, which were loud and long, and ceased, according to one eye witness, only when the vast concourse was hoarse. This was one of the few occasions in the long and distinguished career of John Clifford when he was overcome by the reception accorded him, but, as ever, he rose to the occasion and delivered one of those impassioned orations which have made his name famous for all time in the annals of the Free Churches. Passive Resistance, he said, had come to stay whether the government liked it or not, and he reaffirmed the determination of Free Churchmen to fight on.

At Hastings and Bury St. Edmunds, unfortunate scenes developed at "distraint" sales. At Hastings, the police admitted that Passive Resisters were not to blame, while at Bury in a crowd of over five hundred involved in the incident there were only fifteen resisters. It would seem that Clifford was right when he claimed that such scenes were an exhibition of indignation by people affronted by an Act distasteful to them.

A new stratagem soon appeared on the scene. At Maidenhead, a local councillor paid all the outstanding rates of Passive Resisters in order to avoid unpleasant scenes and possible indignation meetings. Similar events took place at Carlisle and Poole, while the Lord Mayor of Sheffield, who had refused to pay the rate, had it paid for him by an anonymous friend. Passive Resisters responded to this device by instructing the overseer not to accept payment of the rate from any other person.

Throughout the summer of 1903, resistance increased steadily, and the situation was one which fully justified the misgivings of the Archbishop of Canterbury. Worse was to follow, however, for the Cambridgeshire County Council followed the example set by the Welsh County Councils,[1] and refused rate aid to schools not fully under popular control, and to schools where teachers were still subject to religious tests.

In January 1904, a Passive Resisters' Anti-Martyrdom League was formed in Bradford with the express purpose of preventing respected citizens making themselves ridiculous by trying to achieve cheap martyrdom. The League therefore aimed at paying all the outstanding rates which Resisters had refused. This was an unfortunate and regrettable incident, for it increased the feeling which the controversy had evoked on both sides. Free Churchmen were, not unnaturally, most indignant at such a cheap and insolent sneer aimed at men who were intent on obeying the higher law of conscience. This League demonstrated the fact that in some quarters there was an utter and lamentable ignorance of the issues involved.

[1] *Free Church Chronicle*, July, 1903, p. 178, and August, 1903, pp. 203–204. Article "Working the Act to Kill the Act."

The result of the London County Council elections in March 1904 turned out to be another heavy blow for the government, because in most cases Progressives were returned with sweeping majorities despite the fact that some organizations of the Established Church had put in considerable work to try to keep the Progressives out. It was now becoming clear that the result of a General Election would probably go against the government, very largely on the issue of Education. The London elections must have disturbed Mr. Balfour a good deal, for not only did they provide a pointer to the swing of public opinion, but also suggested that the London County Council might be following the example of the Welsh and Cambridge County Councils.

The National Free Church Council, held at Newcastle in March 1904 under the presidency of the Rev. F. B. Meyer, drew up a policy for National Education. This is important because it made a considerable appeal beyond the confines of the Free Churches. Its main points were:

1. There should be one type of elementary school controlled by a public educational authority.
2. Denominational school buildings, if required for use as provided schools, should be rented on equitable terms for elementary education.
3. All schools maintained by public funds should be under the sole control of popularly elected representatives.
4. There should be no religious tests in the appointment and training of teachers.
5. There should be no denominational teaching in elementary schools during school hours. Instead there should be simple Biblical instruction, subject to a conscience clause.

This policy may have been far-reaching in its intentions and, accordingly, outside the immediate practical possibilities, but at any rate it served to answer those who considered the Free Church position to be one of mere negative objection. Here was a sincere attempt to state their position in terms not incongruous in a democratic society.

About this time, the Free Church Council committed itself to a far-reaching decision. After much heart searching and contemplation, the Council decided that it must take the earliest opportunity of expressing, in the manner provided by the Constitution of the State, its resolute disapproval of government policy. It was not easy for the Council to take this step, for its purposes were mainly spiritual, and in the normal course of events it could have nothing to do with matters political, but it was felt that the situation was an extraordinary one necessitating extraordinary measures. The National Executive therefore decided to fight the next General Election. The immediate result of this decision was twofold. Firstly, a deputation waited on the Liberal Party leaders and was assured by Mr. Asquith and Mr. Herbert Gladstone that if the Liberals were returned at the next election they would take steps to accomplish a fair and a just settlement of the Education question. The second result was that a Free Church Council Election Fund Appeal for £50,000 was launched. Rightly or wrongly, the decision was taken and the Council, while establishing no organic link with the Liberal Party, practically committed itself to work for a Liberal victory at the polls. Circulars were sent out to all Free Church ministers and to many influential laymen appealing for generous support. A promise of £5,000 was soon forthcoming from Mr. W. P. Hartley, head of the Liverpool jam firm, and one of £2,500 from George Cadbury.

Detailed plans were laid for intensive house-to-house canvass and for the distribution of a great mass of literature once the election came in view. Elaborate arrangements were made for tightening up the already efficient organization of the local Councils, and Thomas Law soon showed that here he was in his element. An acquaintance has described Thomas Law as a consummate organizer, and a man to whom the Liberal victory of 1906 owed more than has ever been recorded. Thomas Law communicated with many prominent Free Churchmen urging them to stand for Parliament and promising them financial support wherever possible. A mass of literature poured forth from the Council Press and was circulated to every conceivable contact. One example is worth our notice. It was quite a little booklet, entitled *Organizing for Elections*, and it was for the perusal and guidance of local Council secretaries. Into this unusual publication, Thomas Law poured all his vast experience of organization for the benefit of the key men in the great campaign to overthrow the Tory Government. Soon afterwards the Council were able to stage a real rehearsal, for at a bye-election at Norwich, in which the Council participated, the seat was won from the government, while at the Mid-Herts election, Mr. J. Bamford Slack, a prominent Free Churchman, was returned as a Liberal in what had been considered a safe government seat. Results like this stimulated and encouraged Thomas Law and his supporters, but for the government it was the writing on the wall.

In March 1904 two ministers were committed to prison for non-payment of the Education rate. The Rev. Allon Poole of Southgate was sentenced to seven days' imprisonment, but escaped because someone paid the rate for him, while the Rev. W. H. Higgins of Coventry spent seven days in Warwick Gaol, for in order to avoid distraint upon his goods he had made them all over to his wife.

In July 1904 there was a new development at Scarborough. The overseers refused to distrain or to recover the rate but warned the offenders that unless the money was paid by a certain time, their names would be removed from the electoral register. The eventual result was that fifty-six people were disenfranchised, including eight Free Church ministers, an ex-alderman and an ex-councillor. Similar drastic action appears to have been taken at Hereford, while at Taunton, Mr. Penny, J.P., a former Mayor, was threatened in similar vein. In September, however, the Revising Barrister for North-East Lancashire ruled that non-payment of the Education rate, or part of it, should not disqualify a voter, and, thereafter, with a precedent established, threats of disenfranchisement disappeared from the struggle.

By the autumn of 1904 the Passive Resistance movement had made considerable advances and was assuming a character and proportions that could not be ignored. The government had no doubt pushed the Act through in the hope that the initial anger of Free Churchmen would quickly burn itself out, and that they would soon become reconciled to a *fait accompli*. The government did not envisage organized opposition nor, when that opposition appeared, were they unduly alarmed, for they felt that this too would quickly spend itself. We do not know how far the government was influenced by the personal opinion of Mr. Balfour, but that he sadly miscalculated the situation is now perfectly clear. By the autumn of 1904 with resistance still spreading appreciably, the government was beginning to realize that the situation was serious, and daily becoming more disturbing. Time had not blunted the sharp edge of Free Church anger, and many on the government benches viewed the future with misgivings. The gamble had failed and the bill had still to be presented.

It is not surprising, therefore, to find about this time a perceptible, significant, and, on the whole, a general change in the attitude of the magistracy to Passive Resisters when they appeared in court. There were fewer peremptory and harsh dealings; generally every courtesy was extended to the offenders; and often the Bench expressed open admiration and sympathy. Men whose names were household words in the religious world continued their protests before the authorities—men who were not seeking cheap notoriety but who believed that the Education Act violated those sanctities in life and conscience which legislation has no right to invade. Responsible men and women were beginning to realize more and more the deep spring of these continued protests. The old cheap and insolent sneers were less frequent, and many began to realize that the "dissidence of dissent" was not just an affected policy of obstruction and obstinacy but a stand for freedom in the Educational sphere which no man, Bishop, Judge, Tory or peasant could afford to ignore. And so, gradually, the status of the Passive Resister changed. He was no longer thought of so much in terms of an "anti-nomian rebel" but more in terms of the representative of a growing body of free opinion.

One of the most famous figures in Free Church life, Dr. Campbell Morgan, appeared before the Croydon magistrates for refusal of the rate in March 1905, and on the following Sunday he delivered his apologia at Westminster Chapel, thrilling a mighty congregation with an impassioned defence of the liberty of the soul. Dr. Campbell Morgan was a much respected and beloved figure far beyond the confines of his own denomination, and the witness of men of his calibre could not help but create the greatest impression far and wide.

At Leicester some two hundred and fifty of the best-known citizens appeared before the magistrates, and it is interesting to note that among them was the Deputy Mayor, the Liberal candidate for Melton, a Church of

England Town Councillor, a son of the Mayor, and many Free Church ministers and councillors. The greatest courtesy was afforded them in public.

During the months of April and May 1905, the government attempted to enforce the Local Authorities' Default Act. This measure had been passed largely because the Welsh County Councils had been administering the Education Act without using the local rates to support denominational schools. After the passing of this measure, the County Councils responded by attempting to administer the denominational schools so economically from government grants that local rate aid was unnecessary. Again, they refused rate aid to these schools, many of which were in a sorry condition, until their buildings had been put into a satisfactory state of repair and efficiency. By February 1905 the Welsh Councils claimed that still no rate aid had been given to voluntary schools, yet the government had not used their exceptional powers under the Default Act. When the government did at last retaliate bitter indignation was stirred up in Wales and the Welsh authorities still insisted on proper repairs and conditions in the denominational schools as a necessary qualification for rate aid, and, in any event, the government was becoming increasingly uncertain of itself and was in no position to rouse further opposition, so that the Default Act was not pressed home as severely and uncompromisingly as it might have been.

Throughout 1905 Passive Resistance continued to spread. New faces were appearing constantly to reinforce the solid ranks of the veterans, and in September record figures were established. By October 1905 there had been over two hundred and thirty imprisonments.

It was obvious to any discerning eye that the country was moving remorselessly towards a crisis. The government was being openly challenged and defied by methods which were becoming intensified rather than diminished. At the Memorial Hall, Thomas Law and his henchmen went ahead with their preparations for the inevitable. Literature, funds, public meetings, electoral registration, lists of speakers, vehicles—in fact everything which was relevant to the efficient fighting of an intensive election campaign—all received careful and competent attention and preparation. This great electoral machine went into action at a number of bye-elections and contributed substantially to Liberal victories at Devonport, Sowerby, West Monmouth, Stalybridge and North Dorset.

Something dramatic and eventful had to happen, and it came on December 4, 1905, when Mr. Balfour's government resigned, and amid mounting excitement and tension Sir Henry Campbell Bannerman, the leader of the Liberals, responded to the King's summons by accepting office and forming a government without appealing to the country. The Unionist Party had held office for some twenty years, excepting a brief spell between 1892 and 1895, when the Liberals were in office but hardly in power.

The causes of the downfall of Mr. Balfour need not delay us overlong. To claim that the Education controversy and Passive Resistance were the main factors involved would be historically incorrect, but there is no doubt that they played a most important part. Many factors combined to achieve the government's downfall. There was, for example, a split within its own ranks, caused by Mr. Chamberlain's vigorous campaign in the country for Tariff Reform and Imperial Preference. A group of convinced Free Traders in the Cabinet considered that Mr. Balfour should repudiate the views of Mr. Chamberlain, while, on the other hand, a pro-Chamberlain group pressed for action. Mr. Balfour, who had succeeded Lord Salisbury as Prime Minister in 1902, had the unenviable task of trying to keep both sections together, and ended up, so it would seem, by pleasing no one. Other contributory reasons for the fall of the government are not hard to find. There was abroad in the country a disillusionment after the imperialist enthusiasm of the nineties; there was a vague but growing demand for measures of social reconstruction which had met with no real satisfaction; and there was also great dissatisfaction with recent government legislation, and here, Free Church Council opposition to the Education Act, and the fact that the Council and the Passive Resisters had kept the matter vividly before the public eye for more than three years, played a most important part. Apart from Nonconformist opposition, the Education Act had seriously displeased the general body of electors because of the extra burden on taxes and rates. Free Church resistance did much to sum up and make articulate a very considerable area of discontent.

The government had also agreed, under pressure from the Rand mine owners in South Africa, to sanction the recruiting of indentured Chinese coolies to work in the gold mines. The Chinese were more amenable than black workers and far less costly than the white. This aroused great indignation against the Balfour government and evoked cries of "Chinese Slavery". Here again, and in relation to the Licensing Bill of 1904, the Free Church Council played an important part in opposing the legislation and voicing the indignation of many millions of Englishmen. One may say, therefore, that while there were many factors involved in the downfall of the Balfour government and the subsequent remarkable result of the Election in 1906, the Free Church Council played no small part by its resolute and prolonged resistance to government measures which had violated the Nonconformist, and indeed a much wider, conscience.

The country soon had an opportunity of expressing its

opinion on Mr. Balfour's government, for a General Election was held early in 1906. This turned out to be one of the most sensational in the history of British parliamentary government, for the Unionists were swept aside by one of the most sudden and complete reversals of political fortune. Mr. Balfour's majority of 74 was converted into a parliamentary minority of 356, and the catastrophe was completed for Mr. Balfour personally, when he was defeated in his own seat at Manchester which he had held for over twenty years. Discredited in the country, rebelled against by factions within his own party, it was indeed a bitter hour for the Tory Premier, and it says much for his courage and spirit that, in the moment of utter disaster, he could accept the present and face the future undismayed.

It may be of some interest to quote the actual figures for this Parliament, which Free Churchmen everywhere welcomed with eager anticipation and rejoicing: 157 Conservatives were returned; 85 Irish Nationalists, who were to give steady support to the Liberals; 377 Liberals; and—a very significant feature—51 members of the new Labour Party. The Liberals therefore had an overall majority of over 80, and with their allies, could outnumber the Conservatives by over three to one.

It was abundantly clear, therefore, that the Conservative government had outstayed its welcome and that the country was firmly resolved on a change of policy. We may notice in passing the ominous shadow cast by the permanent and overwhelming majority of the Tories in the House of Lords. The Upper House could, if it was bold enough, reduce the great majority of the Commons to impotence, and this, from the first, in view of the bitter political opposition of these two great majorities, rendered a major constitutional conflict inevitable.

The story of the 1906 Election is not complete, however,

without a closer look at the actual part played by the Free Church Council. As soon as it was known that a General Election was on the way, the Council issued a manifesto which was circulated by the million and which embraced the following important points:

1. The need for a completely national educational system under effective public control.
2. The need for immediate Temperance Reform owing to the inadequacy of the Licensing Bill.
3. The need for prompt action in the matter of Chinese indentured labour in South Africa.
4. The need for effective attention to the serious and urgent social problems of the nation.

Clearly, the appeal of this manifesto was not confined to Free Churchmen. It found a ready response in the thought and hopes of many who believed that a Liberal government would be far more competent and willing to deal with such problems than a Tory one would. This manifesto embraced reasonable policy and it was excellent electioneering.

The Free Church Council forces during the election campaign were disposed according to the greatest need, and energies were not wasted where success was more or less assured. The organization behind it all can only be described as absolutely first class. Important conferences were held at centres such as London, Manchester, Leeds and Birmingham for all Federation secretaries. Rapid surveys of every constituency were made and detailed hints and suggestions were given to these secretaries, who were then despatched to brief the local Council secretaries and leaders. Final "whip" circulars were issued in which all instructions and plans were summarized. Some of these were printed in card form for hanging on the wall so that local Council officials could be reminded at a glance of what needed doing. Nothing was forgotten, overlooked or neglected. The master brain of Thomas Law, the consummate organizer, directed, controlled and sustained a campaign worthy of any modern political machine.

Many Free Church leaders undertook extensive motor tours in the interests of the election campaign. The Rev. F. B. Meyer was one of them. In the company of the Rev. Thomas Yates of Kensington, he toured the Western counties, and both have left us the record of their impressions. F. B. Meyer tells us that:

> The conspicuous and outstanding feature of the tour was the perfectness of the organization of our great Free Church Federation . . . the network is more than a paper scheme.

Thomas Yates commented:

> One impression was constantly being repeated and enforced. It was of the extraordinary range and influence of the Free Church Council movement.

Dr. Clifford and Dr. Campbell Morgan toured the Eastern counties, while Silvester Horne and the Rev. J. D. Jones covered the South-West Midlands. Dr. Campbell Morgan tells us that:

> Never before have I felt so thankful for Free Church Federation, or so sure that it has been one of the greatest Divine gifts to the Church.[1]

These, and many others of the most capable platform speakers of the Free Churches, toured the country summoning the electors to vote only for those candidates who would pledge themselves to the main points of policy laid down in the manifesto of the Council. It is true that they called for a Liberal victory and were a most effective part of Liberal Party propaganda, not because the movement was a political caucus but because they sincerely and

[1] *Free Church Year Book 1906*, pp. 190f.

passionately believed that the interests of the Kingdom of Christ could best be promoted and served, under the prevailing circumstances, by a Liberal victory at the polls.

Free Church Council demonstrations were staged at all the large provincial centres, and the outstanding leaders of Nonconformity rallied to the standard. A huge central demonstration was held in the Queen's Hall in London where John Clifford, John Scott Lidgett and Percy Bunting took part. Dr. Rendel Harris, J. H. Jowett, Joshua Rowntree, the Rev. John Wilson of Woolwich, Principal Ritchie, and Dr. Paton were but a few of a host of prominent Free Churchmen who rendered yeoman service and who made the campaign a startling success.

This great campaign then furnishes us with ample proof of the extensive and efficient organization which Thomas Law had built up, perfected and controlled for over ten years. It covered the whole country and was effectively adapted to the needs of a political campaign. It is, of course, impossible to estimate with any degree of accuracy what share in the Liberal victory can be assigned to this Free Church Council activity. One thing is quite certain, however. Its success must have been considerable, even when full allowance has been made for the other causes which contributed to the sweeping defeat of the Tories. There were one million Free Church voters,[1] at least, in the country, capable of a wide influence, and most of them indignant with a government which had flaunted their wishes and affronted their principles. No doubt there were some Free Churchmen who voted Tory or Labour, but the overwhelming majority were solidly behind the Liberals. Moreover, the intensive propaganda of the Council and the undoubted appeal and influence far beyond the Free Churches of men like John Clifford, Campbell Morgan and F. B. Meyer, each of whom

[1] Women, of course, did not vote in 1906.

"electioneered", coupled with the acceptability of the Council's Election Manifesto, must have won a very considerable response from that "floating" vote which seems to be the sure key to political fortune. The opinion has been expressed by informed Free Churchmen who lived through those exciting days of 1906, that Thomas Law was the man who, more than any other, contributed to the Liberal victory, and that is not as extravagant a claim as it appears on the surface.

The return of the Liberals in 1906 in such tremendous strength commenced a new era of hope and expectation for the Free Churches in the first decade of the century; but before we close this chapter, it seems necessary to attempt to reach some verdict on the Free Church Council's attitude to the Education controversy, and the practice of Passive Resistance, as well as to examine the Council's participation in a campaign in the interests of one political party. Many hard things have been said on these issues, and the Free Church Council position has not always been understood, so that some effort must be made to sum up these difficult and involved questions.

The first thing to be quite clear about is that none of the activity of the Council in these directions overshadowed or reduced the firm and sustained evangelism of the movement. Much less than justice has been done the Council in this connexion. For example, united Missions were more numerous between March 1902 and March 1903 than in previous years, and Gipsy Smith reported that the attendances and results had been greater than he had ever known before. This was confirmed by other evangelists of the Council who claimed that the evangelical passion engendered by the Simultaneous Missions of 1901 was intensified during this period. In 1904 the story was again one of increased enterprise in the field of evangelism. Gipsy Smith claimed that the year surpassed even the remarkable results of the previous twelve months. 1904 and 1905 showed no slackening. Extensive open-air work as well as the normal type of mission was undertaken all over the country. During 1905, the President, the Rev. Dr. R. F. Horton, held a series of special Conventions in various parts of the country so that at least one Convention might be held within the reach of every Free Churchman. The centres chosen were Plymouth, Llandrindod Wells, Lowestoft, Sunderland, London, Cheltenham and Harrogate. These meetings secured great support and response, and at each centre eloquent testimony was borne to the good that they had accomplished. When due allowance has been made for the natural exuberance of all these testimonies, one cannot help but underline the fact that the Education controversy did not obscure or reduce the main interest and activity of the Free Church Council. During this turbulent period, evangelism increased, and with it, the impact of the Free Churches upon the spiritual life of the nation. This, then, is the basic framework within which the Council's relation to the Education controversy must be set.

As we have already seen, there is no doubt that the new Education Act achieved many admirable improvements. It not only imposed upon the local authorities the duty of providing efficient elementary education, but it also did much to create a coherent system of education leading right up to the universities. Secondary education for the first time received proper financial support and was co-ordinated with the rest of the national system. The new local authority was able to devise broader schemes than the old School Boards had often administered. The Act led to a great enlargement of secondary schools and it created a ladder to the universities for poor students of the requisite ability and this, of course, raised the standard at the universities. The Nonconformist objections, one must admit, frequently failed to appreciate these important facts. Attention centred upon the fact that, if the matter was pressed, Nonconformists were required to pay something towards religious instruction within the voluntary schools which was unacceptable to them, or towards plain undenominational teaching in the State-provided schools where they had no such control as the religious bodies in the voluntary schools enjoyed.

Nonconformists, of course, were not alone by any means in their opposition to the new legislation. A considerable proportion of the general body of electors opposed the new measure because of the additional burden upon the taxpayer, and, subsequently, because of the shameful treatment of some of the worthiest and most respected citizens who felt they must become Passive Resisters. Mr. Chamberlain himself saw the danger, and in a letter to the Duke of Devonshire in 1902, prophesied that the Bill would sow the seeds of an agitation which would be successful in the long run. Again, there were some Anglicans, and amongst them certain influential people, who found it hard to accept the measure. It must be frankly admitted, however, that many zealous Free Churchmen and their "secular" supporters did not make full allowance for the fact that the government were well intentioned, and had made a bold effort to remove long-existing educational disabilities, and to put the whole question on a sound and integrated footing. If the result in the working out of the Act was, in one way, regrettable and disastrous, let it not be forgotten that there was another side to the picture and that the Act established permanently certain admirable principles.

What is more our concern, however, is whether Free Churchmen were justified in offering opposition to the Act to the extent of their refusal to pay the local rate. The Free Church Council did not commit itself officially to

Passive Resistance, but this seemed to be a matter of expediency rather than conviction, and one must admit that probably only a minority of its supporters actually disapproved of Passive Resistance. Many people claimed that the opposition should have been confined to vigorous condemnation and protest, and should not have been carried to the point where steps were taken the logical outcome of which, if adopted by all, would have been chaos and anarchy. Others claimed that taxes, and the payment of them, were supported by New Testament teaching, the implicit understanding being that the State was ordained by God for the peaceful functioning and operation of human life. To refuse to pay taxes to the State was, therefore, tantamount to undermining the essential fabric of social stability. It was a lawless, rebellious act calculated to create more and greater problems than it could possibly solve. This on the one hand.

On the other hand, some replied that this was a matter of conscience. They claimed that the authority of the British Parliament ceased, for them at any rate, when its decrees and actions violated the sanctity of the human conscience. It was no less than a choice between a human law and a higher one, and there could, for them, be no retreat from the supreme duty of obedience to the latter. This is a powerful and compelling argument. Many great advances have been made in the history of the human story, only because men have had the courage to stand out in obedience to their own light and conviction against the conservative forces of law and order. Many examples spring to mind, such as the early martyrs, Martin Luther, and in more recent times, the early Separatists who defied the State prohibition of their conventicles and so brought to birth the Free Church tradition. One could cite many more examples. That conscience is a valid ground for refusing to discharge certain duties which militate against a man's personal convictions is becoming more and more widely recognized, and is evidenced by the far more lenient treatment of conscientious objectors in the Second World War, as compared with the First. The sanctity of conscience is by no means a shallow platitude because it involves the worth of human personality. For example, to cite an exaggerated analogy, there would be millions of active resisters to a government decree which levied a tax upon all citizens, in order to establish, let us say, a national system of brothels. It cannot therefore be said that resistance to authorized decrees is necessarily an act of implicit anarchy, calculated to shatter the foundations of decent and ordered society. On the contrary, in certain circumstances, disobedience and resistance may be a paramount duty in order to keep open the lifelines of progress, freedom, justice and truth. Conscience can be the shining sentinel of society. It seems therefore a matter of circumstance or degree, resistance being justified against reactionary and evil commands.

The question then is whether the Education Act of 1902 was of such malign content, so reactionary, so clearly evil that Nonconformists were justified in refusing to pay the rate? Clearly, even at that time and within the Free Churches, there was no unanimity upon the question. The decision of the Free Church Council not to commit itself officially to Passive Resistance was dictated by a cleavage of opinion amongst its own members. Free Churchmen were practically unanimous in their condemnation of the Act, but many felt that on the same grounds of conscience which prompted their comrades to offer Passive Resistance, they could not bring themselves to withhold the rate. It must be remembered that probably by far the great majority of Free Churchmen did not pay rates and so were not in a position to join the ranks of the Resisters. However, the Free Churchmen who were and who did not, felt that the Education Act, no matter how much they might condemn it or disapprove of it, was not sufficient reason for so serious a step as refusing to pay a rate demanded by the body charged with the maintenance of common order, and the protection of interests and life. They remembered too that the religious or denominational teaching within the voluntary schools was only a fraction of the work accomplished there, the remainder being sound and acceptable. They remembered, doubtless, that Anglican ratepayers would be supporting Methodist schools, and that people who were opposed to religious teaching of any description would be paying the rate as well. Moreover, some of the more discerning ones realized that the attitude of the Passive Resisters was dangerous if pressed to its logical conclusion, for if one was to examine closely the uses for which public money was employed, then an arguable case could be made out for not paying any taxes at all! As George Bernard Shaw has said:

> The Englishman of to-day is crowded into a corner of an Empire in which the Christians are a mere eleven per cent of the population: so that the Nonconformist who allows his umbrella stand to be sold up rather than pay rates towards the support of a Church of England school, finds himself paying taxes not only to endow the Church of Rome in Malta, but to send Christians to prison for the blasphemy of offering Bibles for sale in the streets of Khartoum.[1]

Mr. Shaw's statement is not without its defects,[2] but the logic of his argument is obvious. Where is one going to draw the line? It would, for example, be necessary for a convinced pacifist, on this argument, to refuse to pay his income tax in time of war, but how many sincere pacifists

[1] Preface on the Prospects of Christianity in *Androcles and the Lion* (Constable). Quoted by permission of the Society of Authors.

[2] For example, rates, unlike taxes, are specifically apportioned to their various purposes. There is a distinction here, but one much too fine to base a serious revolt on!

did this in the last war? If the implicit thesis of Passive Resisters was pressed home and carried to its furthest lengths, then government would be most difficult, if not impossible. Free Churchmen were set in a society, and the mere fact that they were members of that society entailed certain inescapable obligations, not the least of which were the financial ones. To repudiate such obligations could only be considered as a very last resort in the face of some extremely grave threat. It was not as if the rate in question was devoted to some militant atheism or paganism. It was levied largely for the support of sound education and for a small fraction of religious teaching in the voluntary schools, but to listen to some of the Passive Resisters, one might have thought that it was to be devoted to the promotion of immoral tenets.

In such manner many Free Churchmen must have argued, for the Resistance movement caused grave concern and strong disapproval in not a few Free Church minds. It was clearly a matter for the individual to decide, and the Free Church Council was wise in refusing to identify itself officially with a movement of which a number of its own supporters disapproved.

It would be an impertinence in many ways for us to condemn the Passive Resistance movement, for that would be to violate the sanctity of the human conscience. We may leave the problem by saying that in an age which is facing much greater issues and far more momentous problems than the Edwardians ever dreamed of, the Passive Resistance movement seems to be a strange phenomenon of a more negative and intolerant Nonconformity than we know to-day.

There remains for our consideration the question of whether the Free Church Council was wise to participate in an election campaign in the interests of a particular political party. When the decision was taken, the Council sought to justify itself with the claim that an extraordinary situation demanded extraordinary measures. To be fair, it is not difficult to understand the seething discontent which the great majority of Free Churchmen felt for the Tory government. They had every reason to desire its speedy removal. Nor is it difficult to understand how they turned naturally to the Liberal Party as the potential champion of their cause. To support the latter as citizens exercising their electoral privilege was the most natural thing in the world under the circumstances, but to support the Liberal Party officially as active members of a great religious Federation was probably a mistake.

It will be remembered that the Free Church Council from its earliest days had taken the utmost care to avoid associating itself with the political action of the Liberation Society, but in 1905 and 1906 Council members apparently had no qualms about taking political action in the matter of education. Moreover, the fact of fighting the election with such vigour and preparation, and one must add—relish, in the interests of one political party, even though there was no organic relationship with that party, gained for the Free Church Council the reputation of being a political caucus with a thin religious veneer—a wolf in sheep's clothing. This was certainly not a true accusation, as an unbiased examination of the facts reveals. The Council, through and in it all, remained primarily a spiritual organization, and the emphasis on Evangelism was never lost nor did such activity diminish, but no one can be blamed for misunderstanding and misinterpreting the nature and aims of the Council after such a magnificent election campaign.

The chief duty of the churches is to promote the interests of the Kingdom of God and to worship God, and the Church cannot ultimately accomplish either of those tasks by championing a single political party, for as the humorous remark once passed, and now famous, tells us—an election means taking one lot of sinners out and putting another lot in! How true! No political system or party is sacrosanct. All are the work of man's hand, and are consequently shot through with his imperfection and self seeking, and while it is correct that the Gospel must be taken into every sphere, including the political, it does not mean that the Church must identify itself with one particular conception or organization. Nor does it mean that Christians need go as "guerrillas", as Dr. Dale had urged. More and more it appears that Christians must go into such departments of life, united as Christians, forming their own parties and organizations if needs be, not emphasizing that their aims happen to coincide with one party, as they did in 1906, but proclaiming the difference of motive within the Christian view, for the simple reason that the Christian motive issues from the life and fellowship of a society not the work of man's hand but of the redemptive activity of God Himself.

Perhaps it is significant that after 1906, although the movement remained vigorous and strong numerically, the influence of the Council never seemed to be quite what it had been. Certain of its supporters began to be less enthusiastic, and others soon began to call for a more authoritative organization.

Now almost fifty years after, we can see both sides of the picture—the compelling reasons why the Council took such action, and the reasons why it might have been wiser to have avoided it. It was an important step and a landmark in the history of the Council. Mistakes as well as triumphs are the stuff of which the chequered tapestry of history is woven.

Chapter 6

RELIGION AND POLITICS

THE advent of the Liberal Government raised Free Church hopes to a remarkable degree. The departure of the Tories seemed to open up the way for the long-desired educational redress, and on every hand there was excitement and expectation. Hopes were further stimulated when Mr. Birrell's Education Bill received its first reading in the Commons in April 1906. Broadly speaking, this Bill aimed at bringing all publicly maintained schools under effective public control. It proposed to abolish all theological tests in the teaching profession and to relieve the taxpayer of the cost of sectarian teaching, thus removing the grievance which evoked Passive Resistance.

The Bill was generally welcomed in Free Church circles, although it was by no means all that the Free Church Council desired. On the other hand, the Anglicans termed it a Nonconformist Bill and were bitterly opposed to it, and, as expected, the Lords proved difficult and produced numerous amendments. A special National Council was summoned in November 1906, this being the first time that the Free Church Council had been specially summoned, and urged the Prime Minister to reject the Lords' amendments *en bloc*. The Commons subsequently obliged and returned the Bill to the Upper House, but the Lords insisted on their objections, and after some abortive negotiations, the Bill was finally withdrawn. The writing was very definitely on the wall, but for the moment the veto of the peers reigned supreme.

About the end of February 1907 Mr. Reginald McKenna, who had taken over from Mr. Birrell at the Board of Education, introduced a new measure. The main object was to abolish the injustice of the 1902 legislation by relieving citizens of the cost of teaching theological creeds and catechisms. The average value of the time spent by a teacher on religious lessons was fixed at one-fifteenth, and the religious authorities in the voluntary schools were asked to provide that proportion of the teacher's salary.

This Bill did not set out to deal with the educational problem as a whole, but aimed at putting an end to Passive Resistance and lessening the tension in the educational world. By May 1907 rumours were circulating to the effect that the Bill was to be quietly dropped in view of the expected Anglican resistance. The Free Churches called on the government to stand firm and implement the promises made when it took office, but despite all efforts, the Bill was withdrawn at the end of May, and the promise of a comprehensive Education measure in 1908 did not altogether restore the confidence of the Free Churches in the government.

John Clifford pointed out that the real trouble was not the good faith of the Liberal Government but the supremacy of clericalism in the Upper House, and he appealed for a great intensification of Passive Resistance to demonstrate the complete determination of Free Churchmen not to rest until victory was won. Clifford, as usual, was right. When the Liberals attempted to implement their promises there ensued either threatened rejection by the Lords, or voluntary withdrawal by the government to save their proposals from humiliating mutilation—and this despite the largest Commons majority in constitutional history. On every hand in the Liberal camp and throughout the Free Churches, and in ever-widening spheres, there was a deepening conviction that the immediate duty was to effect such a readjustment of the constitutional powers of the two Houses, as to allow the will of the people to prevail.

In February 1908 Mr. McKenna had another try. This Bill proposed only one type of school to be supplied out of the rates, namely, the school under the complete control of the local authority where no sectarian teaching could be given during school hours. The Bill thus aimed at making voluntary schools into public elementary schools for five days out of the week, and allowing the buildings to be used for supplementary religious teaching, where desired, on Saturday or Sunday, at the expense of the religious authorities concerned. It was proposed to make a grant of 47s. per annum for every child, the amount needed beyond this in Council schools being levied on the rates, and in denominational schools being found by the managers. The Bill provided a system of contracting out for denominational schools except in single school areas.[1]

The Bill was a bold attempt to resolve the Education problem, and Free Church opinion, on the whole, was favourable, for while the Bill might not be all that was desired, at any rate it gave popular control, the abolition of religious tests for teachers and the removal of the grievance which concerned Passive Resisters.

In April, Mr. Asquith took over from Sir Henry Campbell Bannerman as Premier, but despite new and able leadership, Mr. McKenna's Bill was held up. The Free Church Council leaders, particularly John Clifford, alarmed at the ominous delay in pressing the Bill, warned Mr. Asquith that it might prove impossible to win another election unless government assurances could be translated into concrete results.

In November a possible concordat on Education be-

[1] A single school area was the technical term used for a district where the only available school was a denominational one.

tween the State Church and the Free Church Council was provisionally reached in discussions between the Archbishop of Canterbury and Mr. Walter Runciman, and Mr. Asquith announced in the Commons that in view of this welcome development a new Bill would be drawn up and Mr. McKenna's Bill withdrawn. Suddenly, in the moment of apparent success, difficulties arose over the financial aspect, and strong opposition to the concordat developed in Anglican circles. The representative Church councils showed that the clergy and the laity were strongly opposed to the agreement, and the Archbishop had no option but to bow to the storm. Both Dr. Davidson and Mr. Runciman had to suffer the grievous disappointment of seeing their long and sincere labours brought to nought. Finally, in December 1908, the Bill and Mr. Runciman's proposals were withdrawn.[1]

Again, it had been a year of unfulfilled expectations, but Clifford sent out a stirring call to Passive Resisters to fight on with determination and in increasing numbers. As he pointed out, it was a decided gain that the Archbishop had, by virtue of the negotiations with Mr. Runciman, implicitly acknowledged the unfortunate nature of the 1902 legislation. Dr. Robertson Nicoll threw in his powerful weight with Clifford, in speech and print, and the Resistance movement was strenuously maintained, and both imprisonment and distraint remained common features of English life. In March 1909 the irrepressible Clifford came before the Paddington magistrates for the twentieth occasion. In March 1909 a Conference of Passive Resisters during the Free Church Council assembly at Swansea, took the important decision to reorganize and federate the National Passive Resistance Committee and the Citizens' Leagues into one national Passive Resistance

[1] G. K. A. Bell, *Randall Davidson*, 1935, pp. 522f.; cf. *Free Church Chronicle*, December, 1908, January, 1909.

League. Clifford became president, and James Everett, honorary secretary.

This new and formidable League approved four methods of resistance.

(*a*) Imprisonment.

(*b*) Allowing the law to take its course with distraint of personal goods, but with no repurchase.

(*c*) Similar to (*b*) but with the repurchase of goods.

(*d*) The customary protest before the magistrates followed by payment of the rate in Court.

It seems that by the middle of 1909 the fourth method was the most popular because it satisfied the conscience, gave the least personal inconvenience, and also tended to increase the number of resisters, while remaining a valid and effective protest. Nevertheless, many still preferred to go to prison. By the middle of the year, the Rev. S. J. Ford, Baptist minister at Minchinhampton, had gone to prison for a second spell of fourteen days since the beginning of the year. In Leicester, the Rev. Peter Thomson, another Baptist, suffered regular spells of imprisonment. Indeed, in January 1908 he had been in such poor health due to his incarceration in Leicester Gaol that he was unable to undertake his ministerial duties during the winter. Despite this, Peter Thomson was undaunted in 1909 and persisted in his protests.

Towards the end of 1909 the Free Church Council again warned Mr. Asquith that Free Church grievances were still unredressed, and that unless the Liberals could re-kindle Free Church enthusiasm the prospects of winning the next election were by no means bright. Mr. Asquith rightly pointed out that the blame should be laid at the door of the House of Lords, and he seems to have made the tacit promise that if returned to power, the Liberals would not allow existing injustices and limitations, or the absence of popular control, to continue to deface the system of education. As this promise would have been quite incapable of fulfilment while the veto of the Lords was effective, Mr. Asquith seemed to have faced up to the fact that an election might have to be fought on the specific issue of the constitutional problem.

Shortly after this correspondence, early in December 1909, the Lords committed an unpardonable breach with the custom of the Constitution, and were guilty of usurping the traditional right of the Commons, when they rejected the Budget. No government can govern without the necessary financial support, and accordingly Mr. Asquith advised the King to dissolve Parliament and hold a General Election in January 1910. The Budget, it is true, was an epoch-making one. The reports of the Poor Law Commission marked a new stage in English social life, and the principle of the Budget, broadly speaking, was to transfer the main burden of taxation from the necessities of the poor to the luxuries of the rich, and to employ the total resources of the State for the uplift of the masses.

It was an ominous Budget to those who could discern the signs of the times, for it proclaimed that the twentieth century was to witness a social revolution, and that the age of the common man was dawning. The Budget was the necessary complement of the Report of the Poor Law Commission. The House of Lords, then, in its theoretical position as watchman and auditor of the proposals of the Lower House, may have felt that the Budget was so unusual and startling that the will of the people should be consulted. That is to take a generous view of what the Lords did—they were exercising their traditional custodianship in the interests of the nation as a whole. It is far more probable, however, that the Lords were jealous for their own interests, and that the excuse of wishing to know the will of the people was but a specious pretext to make the position of the government insecure in the hope that the people might react against the Liberals. The fact remains that the Lords laid hands on the dearest and most unquestioned right that the Commons possessed—the right as elected representatives of the nation to tax the people. Even so great a parliamentary lawyer as Sir Frederick Pollock, a Unionist and an opponent of the Budget, declared that the rejection of the Budget by the Peers was the most audacious attempt to subvert the foundations of parliamentary government which had been made since the revolution of 1688. From every point of view, it seems to have been a gross mistake. The bye-elections had begun to turn against the Liberals, suggesting that a Conservative reaction might be on the way. Patience might have secured the desired end, but the Lords would not wait, and,

> . . . at the instigation of the Party leaders, proceeded to commit the greatest tactical error in modern politics.[1]

As G. M. Trevelyan goes on to say, the rejection of the Budget was tantamount, on the part of the Lords, to a claim to force a General Election whenever they wished, for a government unable to raise taxes must resign or be dissolved. The new social consciousness of the twentieth century was hardly the time for the Lords to claim powers which they had not possessed even in the eighteenth century.

Even if they had had no other grievances against the Lords, Free Churchmen were bound by their traditions and principles to fight against the violation of what was a traditional and unquestioned right of Parliament and the people.

The National Free Church Council decided therefore

[1] G. M. Trevelyan, *History of England*, 1945, pp. 704–705.

to enter the political strife of an election campaign once again. The obstructionist tactics of the Lords had impeded and nullified all efforts of the Liberals to implement their promises of 1906. If parliamentary democracy was to be anything other than an empty cliché, it was clear that something had to be done about the Lords. The Council issued a manifesto claiming that the interests of true progress as well as the Free Churches demanded the return of the Liberals. Free Church demonstrations were held all over the country, many notable Free Church leaders, as in 1906, addressed political meetings, and over one and a half million leaflets were issued by the local Councils. A great Free Church Council rally in the Queen's Hall, London, chaired by J. H. Jowett, was addressed by David Lloyd George who, in his own inimitable way, reminded his hearers that all that lay between them and the realization of their dreams, was the veto of the House of Lords.

There were not wanting those who accused the Council of preoccupation with politics. The verdict of history, however, was to be with the Liberals, and there is more than a residuum of truth in the claim that, by their support of the Liberals at this crucial moment in British history, Free Churchmen were serving the wider interests of that eternal Kingdom where no forces of privilege or monopoly hold sway.

The Liberals were returned at the polls with a majority of about 120, the weakness of their position being that it was a composite majority largely dependent on the Irish members.

By April 1910 Mr. Asquith had introduced his veto proposals to the Commons:

> the absolute veto of the Lords must follow the veto of the Crown before the road can be cleared for the advent of a full-grown and unfettered democracy.

The proposals aimed at depriving the Lords of the power

of amending or rejecting a Money Bill; they provided for the passing into law of any measure passed by the Commons in three successive sessions irrespective of what the Lords might do; and they proposed to limit the duration of Parliament to five years. The veto proposals passed the Commons with a comfortable majority, and at the end of April, Lloyd George's Budget passed the Lords and received the Royal Assent. The passing of this Budget, the first effort on a large scale to combat social evils in this way, was a signal victory for the government, but the constitutional struggle was not yet over. It was obvious that the final trial of strength could not long be delayed, but early in May, the death of King Edward VII and the accession of King George V effected a temporary truce in the political situation. There followed the famous veto conferences between four Cabinet Ministers and four members of the Opposition, at the instigation of the new King, in the hope that an amicable solution might be found. By November, these conferences had broken up without agreement,[1] and Mr. Asquith for the second time in twelve months advised the King to dissolve Parliament, and another appeal was made to the electorate.

Once again the Free Church Council supported the Liberal Party, and in a manifesto outlining the gravity of the crisis between the government and the Lords, stressed that some way must be found for the will of the people to prevail. Numerous leaflets were again circulated by the local Councils, and Free Churchmen rallied to fight their third campaign within five years.

Early in December 1910 the country returned the Liberals to power, this time with a majority of 126, and Mr. Asquith was in an unassailable position. As the *Spectator* put it:

> If the Government insists on taking their full pound of flesh, they cannot be prevented from doing so.

[1] Over twenty conferences were held, but complete deadlock resulted.

It was clear that the will of the people, twice expressed, had to prevail. Had the Lords thrown out the Veto Bill and the King declined to create new peers, Mr. Asquith needed only to resign. Mr. Balfour could hardly take office and would not have dared to dissolve Parliament. The King would then have had to recall Mr. Asquith and accept him on his own terms. Happily, any such complications were avoided. Mr. Asquith in July 1911 warned the Lords that should they persist in amending the Bill, the King would take the advice of his ministers and secure that the Bill become law. Warned by Lord Morley that if peers had to be created, it would be done in hundreds, the Lords finally passed the Bill in August by a majority of 17. Led by Lord Rosebery and the two archbishops, more than forty bishops and Unionist peers went into the Government lobby, while many others abstained. The long dominance of the House of Lords was broken. It hardly needs to be added that, broadly speaking, throughout the long controversies of these opening years of the present century, the Church of England was ranged behind the Conservative Party, and Free Churchmen, for the most part, solidly behind the Liberals.

In the meantime, Passive Resistance had continued unabated, and the stalwarts remained undaunted. The Rev. P. T. Thomson of Leicester had been in prison on eight occasions by 1910 for non-payment of the rate. The Rev. S. J. Ford of Minchinhampton figured in the most spectacular incident of the whole campaign when in April 1910 he was sentenced by the Chairman of Nailsworth Petty Sessions to two months' imprisonment for non-payment of a 1s. 9d. rate! Such was the uproar that intervention by the Home Secretary was rumoured, and the Nailsworth magistrates found it necessary to issue a circular defending their action. One of the magistrates was so disturbed that he surreptitiously paid the rate himself, and Mr. Ford was released from Gloucester Gaol. John Clifford, in December 1912, made his thirty-fifth appearance before the Paddington magistrates.

Free Churchmen were, of course, hopeful that with the veto of the Lords removed, the Liberals would press home some kind of solution to the educational problem, but in 1912 a Single School Area Bill was withdrawn after determined opposition from Anglican quarters. In July 1913, Mr. Pease's education proposals were introduced, but after much discussion and delay these were eventually laid aside on the outbreak of war. It was clear, as John Clifford rightly pointed out, that the government knew what the Liberal electorate wanted, but the government had to hold together, and the plain fact was that agreement on education had not been found possible amongst the Coalition parties.

When war broke out, the question was naturally asked, "Shall we proceed with Passive Resistance?" In September 1914, the Resistance Committee came together and favoured continuance of the protest, and this was confirmed in March 1915 at the Annual Meeting of the Resistance League. It was claimed that resistance would not in any way hinder or reduce the war effort, and that, in any case, war or no war, legislation detrimental to the promotion of liberty in the field of religion should be opposed.

This evidence seems to be fairly conclusive in pointing to continued resistance, but a certain little booklet which was brought to the present writer's attention tells a different story. In *A Brief Sketch of the Career of the Rev. F. Cowell Lloyd*,[1] the author claims that soon after the outbreak of war Mr. Cowell Lloyd received a three-page telegram from John Clifford recommending the merging

[1] Len S. Nembard, *A Brief Sketch of the Career of the Rev. F. Cowell Lloyd, A.T.S.*, n/d, pp. 7f.

of Passive Resistance into the one great protest against tyranny which was involved in the unsheathing of the sword. This, claims the author, became the generally accepted policy. Credence is given to this claim, because in actual fact Passive Resistance declined considerably during the war, to say the least.[1] T. H. Darlow tells us:

> The outbreak of the Great War practically made an end of Passive Resistance. To their honour, be it recorded that stalwart Nonconformists forgot everything else in face of the tremendous national emergency.[2]

Many took the view, no doubt, that if the war was lost there would be no liberty at all, or chance of it, so that one should concentrate on the greater evil and postpone dealing with the lesser until later.

It seems that in general T. H. Darlow is correct but not entirely, for John Clifford continued regular protests and came before the magistrates for the fiftieth time, along with several others, in September 1916, and it is possible to trace meetings of the Passive Resistance League as late as 1922. Clifford went on making his protest long after the war ended. It hardly seems therefore that he could have sent such a telegram to Mr. Cowell Lloyd unless he was speaking *ex officio* as Chairman of the League and not as an individual.

The main facts are quite clear however. Clifford and certain others continued their protests, but the war, to all intents and purposes, dealt the knock-out blow to Passive Resistance. It was difficult to convince the great majority of the importance and urgency of such a protest when the nation was fighting desperately for life itself against a ruthless and determined foe. After the war, those who had intended resuming Passive Resistance found such a changed

[1] I am relying chiefly upon the testimony of Free Churchmen who lived through those days. There seems to be substantial agreement on the point.

[2] T. H. Darlow, *W. Robertson Nicoll*, 1925, p. 382.

world, fraught with all the perplexities of transition and aftermath, that they abandoned their resistance.

Mr. H. A. L. Fisher's Education Act became law on August 8, 1918. This Bill had been earnestly supported by the Free Church Council, for it represented a considerable development of the elementary system. It refused exemption from attendance at school between the ages of 5 and 14; it prohibited employment under the age of 12; and it compelled the medical inspection of schools and the development of physical education. It did not, however, remove the grievances upon which Passive Resistance was founded, and in 1919, the Free Church Council tempered its welcome for the Bill with a plea for further legislation.

In the post-war world, the outcry against the 1902 Act died away. The two main reasons are admirably explained by G. M. Trevelyan.[1] In the first place, the control exerted by the county educational authorities over Church schools proved more effective than the majority of Nonconformists had anticipated. The 1902 Act transferred the direction of religious instruction from the exclusive control of the parson to the authority of the school managers, thus opening up the way for the Agreed Syllabus which has done so much towards solving the problem of religious teaching in schools. Secondly, the general attitude to religious controversy has altered much in the last few decades. The steady drift away from religion, and the rapid inroads of modern paganism, caused tempers to cool, prejudices to disappear very largely, and brought to birth a new spirit of co-operation and a recognition that there were more important issues to fight for than the Education rate.

Christians have become kinder to one another, and the Church of England clergy no longer regard themselves as

[1] G. M. Trevelyan, *History of England*, pp. 693f.

the rulers of society. As G. M. Trevelyan points out, in our own age a reassortment of political parties has taken place on the basis, not of religion, but of varying social and industrial theories. New Radicals have appeared in the shape of the Labour Party—hence the eclipse of the Liberals. The excitement over the Balfour education proposals was the last party fight based upon the political alignments of Dissent and Church.

Chapter 7

TOWARDS A UNITED FREE CHURCH

IN 1912 the Free Church Council pledged itself to a searching Free Church Inquiry. This decision was really the outcome of a remarkable speech by the Rev. J. H. Shakespeare, the Secretary of the Baptist Union, two years earlier, when he pleaded with impassioned eloquence for a United Free Church of England.

He had suggested that a beginning might be made in terms of a United Board to supervise a redistribution of Free Church resources and to undertake wide social and evangelistic service. Once, claimed Shakespeare, the greatest contribution the Free Churches were able to make to the Kingdom of God had been division and separation, but the hour had come when a United Free Church, purged of inessentials and rivalry, could strike a mighty blow for the salvation of England. Shakespeare poured all the passion and intensity of his conviction into his appeal and his hearers were deeply moved. Here, they felt, was a man of vision, a prophet of unfaltering courage like Jeremiah of old with a consuming fire within him. Shakespeare developed his proposals in the pages of *The Christian World*, and other great leaders like Charles Brown, Silvester Horne, Scott Lidgett, J. H. Jowett and Peter Forsyth quickly rallied to his side.

Shakespeare suggested that the Free Church Council should be the intermediary stage between the denominations and the United Board, an idea similar in intention to the one originally in the minds of Charles Berry and

Hugh Price Hughes. There was need for an authoritative clearing house for common problems which were the concern of all the Free Churches, and the Free Church Council, despite its influence and its undoubted achievements, did not possess the necessary authority.

It was clear that the Free Churches were aware, as they felt their way forward into the new century, that new and powerful forces were at work amongst humanity, and that sectarianism, whilst it might achieve joint action and co-operation in a Free Church Council, was by no means an ideal or perhaps a worthy advertisement of Christianity likely to be able to face and harness the new forces. More and more people who, like Shakespeare, were ardent supporters of the Council and who were the first to acknowledge its mighty achievements, were alive to the fact that the time had come when a more authoritative and official body was needed to take more positive and weighty action on matters of common interest and necessity. The way to federation was opening up, and in 1912 few people would have cared to predict that seven long years would elapse before even this limited goal was to be reached.

The Free Church Inquiry committees were instituted in 1913 to make detailed investigations and made a good deal of progress in the early part of 1914, but the investigations were considerably affected by wartime conditions, and had not a further stimulus been forthcoming, they might well have petered out. The stimulus came in Shakespeare's presidential address to the Free Church Council at Bradford in 1916, and it must surely go down in history as one of the most brilliant and penetrating papers ever delivered by a Free Churchman. When he sat down after a truly wonderful oration he was confronted with a remarkable and spontaneous acclamation of the whole, uprising assembly. It is impossible to read this address to-day without being deeply moved, for its appeal and beauty have lived on through the years, but how tremendous it must have been with Shakespeare's burning passion permeating its language. Some of its more thought-provoking passages demand a place in our story:[1]

> We may be called by God to turn our back on our own past. To cling to great names and vested interests and formulae may be to forswear the control of the Living God for the dead hand. There will certainly come a time in our experience when a demand or message in sharp contradiction to all that has gone before will present itself with divine authority before our startled consciousness. . . .
> . . . The feeling is advancing with the inevitableness of the dawn and the springtime, that the differences between the Evangelical Free Churches are not sufficient ground for separation. . . . Denominationalism is a decaying idea—it certainly does not commend itself to a nation in a socialistic age, nor to the very people upon whom its success depends. . . .

Shakespeare claimed that Free Church divisions were ineffective and productive of enormous waste, causing the Free Churches, though large in numbers, to be proportionately weak in their impact upon the nation's life for the simple reason that full strength could nowhere be applied to a single point. The first step, as he saw it, would be in terms of Federation, and he therefore appealed to the Free Church unions and conferences to appoint their ablest men to act on a Federated United Board to explore the possibilities of Free Church Union. Anticipating the objection that uniformity was not desirable, Shakespeare said that there was nothing so uniform and narrow as a denomination, and that a United Free Church with such lively and varied emphases as Baptists, Methodists, Congregationalists and Presbyterians would contribute, could never be in danger of a dead uniformity, but would widen

[1] *Free Church Year Book 1916*, pp. 9–24.

narrow horizons and enrich and hearten all Free Churchmen. Shakespeare well knew that his views would not be acceptable everywhere and that there would be inevitably collision with vested interests, sentiment and family traditions, some reputable, some contemptible, but, he said:

> if we are to be dominated by the narrowest and smallest people, and by timorous counsels, no solution can be found.

The address moved on to a mighty climax, as Shakespeare with ardent zeal and compelling word sought to drive home his argument.

> Sterile arguments and platitudes are of no use. We are in a new era of the world's history. Institutions will have to be rebuilt. Millions of men will come back who have faced the realities of life and death. They will have new measurements and new values. The Church which will hold men then will be the one which knows what are the things that matter. . . . The vision is the rebirth of the Free Churches—the shattering of the shell that the mighty spirit may go free, the vision of a Gospel no longer obscured by a false emphasis on secondary matters, but one worth living and dying for . . . To-day I rear upon the battlefield the standard of the United Free Church of England. Let all ready to do battle for the cause, gather beneath its folds. . . . I appeal to the veterans whose names could be a pledge of victory; I appeal to the younger men whose courage has not yet spent itself in the long assault upon the ramparts of inertia and prejudice.

Shakespeare, however, was not content with oratorical triumph. He knew that the only catholicity worth the name springs not from a loose uniformity but from deep and sincere conviction. A victory won in the Parliament of the Free Churches needed confirmation by the rank and file of Free Churchmen. The omens were indeed propitious. Throughout the country the reception accorded to his proposals had been encouraging. There were articles in the leading daily newspapers; a lively correspondence developed in some publications, and the majority of religious papers responded favourably. The next step was, therefore, to employ the Free Church Council machinery all over the country in order to press home the victory as quickly as possible. The Council press printed and circulated thousands of copies of this memorable presidential address, and Shakespeare himself set out on an extensive Free Church pilgrimage. Everywhere the story was the same—immense crowds packing halls and churches. Not since the days of the pilgrimage of Charles Berry, Hugh Price Hughes and Thomas Law twenty years earlier had the Free Churches known such gatherings and comparable enthusiasm. Shakespeare covered the whole country, visiting over forty Federations as well as numerous local Councils and churches, and at the end of it all he could say:

> There cannot be the least question that the people are with the movement. They are convinced and they are impatient for action. They are tired of inertia and delay. This verdict has come from the members of every denomination.[1]

Shakespeare also toured the Free Church assemblies and annual gatherings in order to state his case in person and to seek each denomination's approval in the appointing of official delegates to a joint conference for the examination in detail of the prospects of Federation. Everywhere he was cordially welcomed, and all the resolutions appointing the representatives were practically unanimous. The Wesleyan Conference was regarded as the greatest hurdle on account of the many cross currents within the denomination. Wesleyans, generally speaking, had been the least enthusiastic in their support of the Free Church Council, there being a large number of Wesleyans who were strong supporters of the Tory Party. It was not

[1] *Free Church Year Book 1917*, p. 15.

without good reason, therefore, that the visit to the Wesleyan Conference was regarded as the Spion Kop of the campaign. Shakespeare and R. F. Horton, who accompanied him, made a great impression, and they were strongly supported by Scott Lidgett, Sir Robert Perks, Dr. Banks and Arthur Henderson, with the result that when the matter went to vote there were only twenty dissentients.

Each denomination appointed ten representatives,[1] and the first conference was held at Mansfield College, Oxford, in September 1916, when committees were set up on such matters as Ministry, Faith, Evangelism, and the Nature of Federation. It is more than likely that the committees set up earlier by the Free Church Inquiry had by now ceased their work owing to the war, but not before voluminous draft reports had come into existence with much valuable information. References to the Inquiry disappear during the war, understandably because conditions were abnormal, and any findings would not have been a true indication of the condition of the Free Churches in normal circumstances. It is almost certain that the work of these committees was taken over by the new Federation committees and that all the results of the Inquiry were placed at their disposal.

Further conferences were held at the Leys School, Cambridge, in March 1917, and in London in the autumn of the same year, when the final touches were administered to an inclusive report and proposals for actual federation. The work of the conferences had been careful and methodical, and the most critical stage of the whole project now lay ahead, for it was by no means a foregone conclusion that the idea of a Federal Council constituted by officially authorized delegates would be endorsed by the denominations. Some denominations, then, as now,

[1] The smaller denominations had two delegates each.

were exceedingly jealous of their autonomy and were greatly suspicious of the new project's intention to interfere with it, while other denominations could be relied upon to resist and even resent the attempt to secure their approval to a declaration of faith. Freedom and independence, so frequently open to abuse by Free Churchmen who were often more bound by tradition than many Anglicans and Roman Catholics, were very real and formidable slogans of the opponents of federation.

In the proposals finally submitted to the denominations there was no attempt to interfere with the autonomy of each federating body. They were proposals designed not for absorption or amalgamation, but for concerted action and economy of resources. No attempt was made to interfere with the distinctive witness and practice of each body, and the statement of Faith, drafted by Dr. Carnegie Simpson, was never designed to be an exhaustive creed but simply a public and corporate testimony.

At the end of April 1918 the proposals came before the Baptist Union. It was a critical moment, for this was the first denominational assembly to face the issue, and Shakespeare, who introduced the proposals to his own people, knew just how much depended on the verdict of the Baptists. Shakespeare was frank and forceful and stated his case eloquently and persuasively:

> this tender little plant lifts its head timidly above the ground after the long winter of sectarianism but it has in it the promise of spring. It says, "Do not mistake me. I am not organic union. I am only a Federation. Do not stamp on me or crush me. Nurture me and surround me with the warm atmosphere of confidence and brotherly love. . . ." Ours is the first denominational assembly to consider the Report. It is unthinkable that Baptists should wreck the movement or even look upon it with distrust and hesitation.[1]

[1] *The Baptist Times*, May 3, 1918.

Charles Brown, speaking in support, used a memorable sentence when he claimed that to refuse to federate would be to forfeit the Baptist claim to be a vital part of the Holy Catholic Church. An amendment, moved by an extreme conservative, to refer the whole question to the local churches and associations particularly with regard to the doctrinal statement, was heavily defeated, and the original motion was carried with only a handful of dissentients. The smallness of the dissenting group was an amazement and a revelation to those who had been alarmed at the vociferousness of the opponents of federation.

So the first hurdle was safely cleared. It has been dealt with in some detail to illustrate the kind of objections with which the Federal scheme had to contend, and to show that, for the most part, federation was acceptable to the large majority, and was opposed mainly by an extremist and unprogressive minority. From these points of view, what happened at the Baptist Union was fairly representative of the other Free Churches with the exception of the Wesleyans.

The resolution pledging the Congregational Union to the Federal scheme, for example, was also carried by an overwhelming majority after one or two amendments had been swept decisively aside. The Primitive Methodists, the Independent Methodists, and the United Methodists accepted the federation proposals with little controversy or delay, and the Moravians, the Wesleyan Reform Union, the Presbyterians, the Disciples of Christ and the Countess of Huntingdon's Connexion followed suit.

In July 1918, however, the Federal scheme suffered a formidable rebuff when the Wesleyan Conference decided to defer the proposals for a year. It was perhaps unfortunate that the matter came up for discussion late on one evening of Conference and, as a result, there was little inclination to afford the proposals adequate discussion. The Rev. J. A. Sharp said that Wesleyans should not go any further along the road to federation, and that many of them were frightened of the new and elaborate organization to be set up. He maintained that the question of overlapping could be competently and sufficiently dealt with by an *ad hoc* commission of Free Churchmen. Sir Robert Perks, guilty of a complete *volte face* from the time when he publicly supported the attempt to bring the churches closer together in such a scheme, took his stand with Sharp. Scott Lidgett, hero of many a stern battle, really saved the day when he showed the deep issues at stake, and pleaded for a responsible and statesmanlike attitude to the subject. He received solid support from Walter Runciman, Luke Wiseman, Dr. Davison and the Rev. John Hornabrook, and the Conference finally agreed to defer the matter for a year. A year later, in August 1919, the Conference again heard J. A. Sharp submit a motion to keep Wesleyans out of the Federal scheme, but the Conference adopted a more gracious and favourable view of federation than hitherto. None the less, Wesleyans were conspicuous by their absence at the first meeting of the Federal Council of the Evangelical Free Churches in October 1919, when this long-awaited, authoritative expression of Free Church unity began its career. Henceforward, the National Free Church Council and the Federal Council of the Evangelical Free Churches were to run on parallel lines before converging and constituting the present Free Church Federal Council in that fateful year of 1940.

Chapter 8

THOMAS LAW—AN ORGANIZING GENIUS

IN April 1910 the Council had suffered a great loss in the death of the Rev. Thomas Law, the able and indefatigable Secretary of the movement for some fifteen years.[1] Hugh Price Hughes, recognizing the ability of Thomas Law, had persuaded him to leave the pastoral ministry to become the full-time Organizing Secretary of the Council. Thomas Law was a consummate organizer and, under his skilful guidance, the Free Church Council grew by leaps and bounds and built up an efficient organization in almost every district of England and Wales. All this was not, however, without price, for the strain of his many duties and responsibilities over his long and arduous period of service took considerable toll of his nervous and mental energy. Insomnia had held him in its exhausting grip for some time, and under the ever-increasing pressure of duties entailed in the education controversy and the succession of General Elections, Thomas Law finally broke down completely, and in a moment of acute and terrible depression, took his own life. So ended in tragic manner a life rich with sacrificial achievement and bright with further promise.

The Free Church Council owed Thomas Law a debt it could never repay. At the crucial and formative stage of its existence, his wonderful organizing ability laid foundations which were to endure, and indeed do so to this day.

[1] The vacancy was filled in the autumn of 1910 by the Rev. F. B. Meyer, who took over temporarily but eventually became permanent Secretary.

He literally worked himself to death in the service of the movement he loved so well.

It is true that he had within the Council not a few critics—people who felt that he was hand in glove with the Liberal Party—but as a leader and organizer everyone agreed that he was unrivalled in his particular duties. When a problem or task arose, Thomas Law was one of those rare and gifted people who could immediately envisage the strategy needed and also the swiftest and most efficient methods of executing that strategy. Men such as Dr. J. C. Carlile[1] have said openly that they did not trust him, and that for the accusations of political preoccupation directed at the Council he must take a good deal of the blame. Be that as it may, and there is some truth perhaps in the suspicions which Law's burning Liberalism encouraged, yet there is another side to the question.

There is no doubt that he used the Council machinery in the interests of the Liberal Party, both in support of many of their bills, and at election times. Indeed, it is probably no overstatement to say that the extent of the Liberal success in 1906 was, in no small measure, due to the energy, efficiency and imagination of Thomas Law. Indirectly, he must have secured thousands upon thousands of those important floating votes upon which the success of political fortunes so largely rests, but it should not be forgotten that he did not browbeat the Council into supporting the Liberals. Men like Clifford, Silvester Horne, J. H. Jowett, J. D. Jones and Campbell Morgan, to mention only a handful, were solidly with him, as were countless thousands of Free Churchmen.

Nor did Law support the Liberals blindly. His ardent championing of their cause was due to the conviction that their ideals and plans were infinitely nearer to the heart of the Kingdom of God than were those of any other

[1] J. C. Carlile, *My Life's Little Day*, 1935, pp. 178f.

political party. For him, Liberal politics sprang from a conscientious root in the soil of true religion. Thomas Law's passion for the Kingdom of God cannot be denied. To read the Annual Reports of the Council is to see his consistent concern for the spiritual depth of the Council's work. To say that he was not to be trusted is to be patently unfair to a devoted and tireless Christian servant, through whose energy, enthusiasm, and personal evangelism, many seekers found the life everlasting.

His tragic end was a bitter shock to Free Churchmen. If ever a man spent himself in selfless service, that man was Thomas Law. Few recall the burdens he bore or the endless journeys he made day after day, and the meetings he so frequently addressed—sometimes three or four in a single day, preceded and followed by a night's travel. When we remember that both Charles Berry and Hugh Price Hughes died prematurely, largely through their endless journeys and endeavours, and that Thomas Law was almost always with them, and that he shouldered increasing responsibilities and burdens in subsequent years, it is not surprising that his nervous energy was finally exhausted, and that, unbalanced and depressed, death offered to him a tempting solution in a moment of acute distress.

J. H. Jowett, in a moving tribute at the funeral, said:

> We remember him as a tireless worker who almost squandered his strength in the service of his Master. I, for one, have no doubt that in his prodigal expenditure of strength was to be found the explanation of the mental infirmity which clouded his last days. . . .
>
> With all my heart—and I feel privileged to say it—I thank God for Thomas Law. . . .[1]

Let that be the last word.

[1] *Free Church Chronicle*, May, 1910, pp. 98–99. In 1902, Thomas Law said, "If I had to die, I should feel that my one great work had been my relation to the Free Church Council."

Chapter 9

THE TRIAL OF WAR

IN June 1914 a neutral observer in England might have had cause for wonder at the perturbing features in the national life. The suffragettes were not content with ordinary methods of persuasion but sought to prove their political maturity by interrupting meetings, smashing windows, chaining themselves to railings, burning down buildings, slashing pictures, to mention only a few of their spectacular escapades. In Ireland, the opponents of Home Rule, the Ulster Protestants, were preparing to offer armed resistance. The Irish Nationalists were preparing for battle as well, while the extreme Catholic Party "Sinn Fein" was suspected of being in relations with Germany. Civil war seemed imminent, and the British Army in Ireland was contemplating mutiny or disobedience if ordered to serve against Ulster. At home, a considerably less antinomian tendency still persisted in the offering of Passive Resistance, and the two great leaders, John Clifford and Robertson Nicoll, were summoning their followers to intensified activity.

Abroad, the international situation seemed easier, with peace in the Balkans and a colonial agreement between Britain and Germany on the verge of completion. Suddenly came terrible news. Archduke Ferdinand, heir to the throne of the Austrian Empire, was assassinated at Sarajevo by a Serb. Austria assumed Serbian responsibility and delivered an arrogant ultimatum, and despite the great and most patient efforts of Sir Edward Grey, backed by France, Italy and Russia, Austria attacked Serbia. Still Grey, the peacemaker, strove to avert a major war, but it was not to be. Russia's mobilization led her into war with Germany, and war between France and Germany automatically followed. Up to the last moment, the attitude of Britain was uncertain. There was a considerable body of opinion within the country which thought it might be possible to keep out of the inferno, and which had influential spokesmen within the Cabinet. All uncertainty was brought to an end, however, when Germany ruthlessly violated neutral Belgium. The King of the Belgians sent a moving appeal to Britain for help, and a British ultimatum to Germany followed. Germany, though now confronted with a formidable alliance, had gone too far to withdraw, and on August 4, 1914, the British people entered with high resolve the most cruel and terrible ordeal of their long history.

There is no doubt that the Great War came as a rude shock to most people. It exploded overnight the easy optimistic theories of inevitable progress, and left multitudes of people stunned, profoundly disappointed, and even resentful. At first, as in the country generally, many Free Churchmen felt that, at any rate, Britain might have kept out of a European squabble. The turning point in Free Church opinion came in November 1914, at a great meeting in the City Temple, under the chairmanship of Dr. Robertson Nicoll. The chief speaker was David Lloyd George who, in his own magic and picturesque way, explained to an audience by no means biased in his favour, why he, a lifelong opponent of militarism, had pledged himself to war. He stated his case clearly and with intense conviction:

> We are in this war from motives of purest chivalry to defend the weak . . If this wanton deed of premeditated treachery against humanity is to pass unchallenged by the nations of

> the world, then let us admit that civilization is a failure, that the sceptre of right is broken, and that force, brute force, is once more enthroned.[1]

The response of his hearers was spontaneous and memorable. The Rev. R. J. Campbell proposed, and John Clifford seconded, a motion which pledged Nonconformity to the fight, and that vast assembly was solidly in favour. Shakespeare, Scott Lidgett, F. B. Meyer, Monro Gibson, and Thomas Phillips were just a few of the leaders who, on that memorable night, added their support. Until that night, it is largely true to say that the Free Churches had been lacking in enthusiasm in their attitude to the war. Henceforward, however, this unmistakable lead was vigorously supported by the great majority of Free Churchmen, and the Free Church Council brought into play its large and efficient network in the interests of extensive relief and welfare work.

The enormous flow of volunteers to the new Kitchener Armies meant that thousands of Baptists, Congregationalists, Primitive Methodists, Welsh Calvinistic Methodists and other Free Churchmen joined the ranks of the new "civilian" armies. David Lloyd George insisted in Cabinet discussions[2] that chaplains should be provided for these Free Churchmen and that they should not be left to the ministrations of the Anglican, Presbyterian or Wesleyan chaplains, all of whom had secure places in Army tradition. It seems that Kitchener stubbornly opposed the idea, but the persistence of Lloyd George won the day, largely because he had the solid backing of the Free Church Council, and in particular of the now famous J. H. Shakespeare, who was a friend of Lloyd George. So eventually the United Board came into being, and an adequate

[1] *Daily News*, November 10, 1914.
[2] Malcolm Thomson, *David Lloyd George: The Official Biography*, n/d, pp. 235f.

number of Free Church ministers of all denominations received service commissions thanks to the vigilance of the Free Church Council, which acted as the clearing house between the military authorities and the Free Churches.

In addition, the repeated and determined representations of the Free Church Council on behalf of Free Churchmen in the Forces resulted in the issue of special instructions from the Army Council to General Officers Commanding to the effect that the statement of his religion by the soldier must be entirely free and uninfluenced, and that existing inaccurate records should be corrected, where desired by the men.[1] Gradually, therefore, the Free Churchman in uniform received increasing recognition on the religious plane, and an excellent example of this was seen in 1918, when the President of the Free Church Council, the Rev. George Hooper, spent a week with the Grand Fleet conducting official Free Church services.

Another service rendered by the Council in these war years was in connexion with conscientious objectors. While recruiting was on a voluntary basis, conscientious objectors did not constitute any problem, but when compulsory military service was introduced in 1916, the Conscription Act provided reasonable concessions for genuine objectors. Tribunals were set up to hear the objections, but if exemption was refused, as it frequently was even in cases of genuine conscience, the unfortunate plaintiff was forced into the Army where, if he disobeyed military orders on conscientious grounds, he was frequently subjected to the most shameful and brutal treatment, and was dealt with by military courts. Again, at the local tribunals, the objector often had to face most unjust and humiliating

[1] In this connexion, appalling ignorance was still shown by Army Record clerks in the 1939–45 war. The recruit, when asked what his religion was, and replying "Baptist" or "Congregationalist" or the like, would sometimes be confronted with the bewildered answer, "Oh! I suppose that's Church of England?" Surely a sign of the times.

treatment. The Free Churches, with their belief in the inviolable sanctity of conscience, took action. A letter was sent in May 1916 from the Free Church Council, signed by J. H. Shakespeare, F. B. Meyer, and J. Scott Lidgett, to the Prime Minister, expressing the strong disapproval and grave concern amongst all the Free Churches at the harsh treatment of conscientious objectors. This letter, whilst expressing disapproval of the attitude of those pacifists who disclaimed any moral right to take part at all in the task and burden of the State and who refused to perform any kind of national service whatsoever, nevertheless called on the government to fulfil the law, which in the Military Service Act had offered reasonable concessions to genuine conscientious objections. The Council demanded uniformity of procedure at all tribunals; the setting up of a Court of Appeal with special qualifications; and the transfer of all men disobeying military orders on grounds of conscience, and those in military prisons for such offences, from the sphere of military discipline to that of the civil courts.[1] There is no doubt that conscientious objectors owed what alleviation of their plight they subsequently received to the influence and energy of the Free Church Council[2], although it is interesting to note that within the Council itself there was a division of opinion on this vexed question. Principal A. E. Garvie[3] tells us that there was a very definite war spirit represented on the Executive of the Council, and that some members had no sympathy at all with conscientious objectors and were unwilling to use the influence of the Council to protect them. These people, however, did not

[1] G. L. Prestige, *Life of Charles Gore*, 1935, pp. 388f., and G. K. A. Bell, *Randall Davidson*, 1935, Vol. II, pp. 817–822, 952–953. It seems that the genuine conscientious objector was transferred in 1916 to the civil power to be directed to work of national importance.

[2] The Quakers had an Independent Committee defending the rights of conscientious objectors.

[3] A. E. Garvie, *Memories and Meanings of My Life*, 1938, p. 169.

win the day, and the Council did much to secure more enlightened treatment for those whose conscience urged that they must contract out of military obligations.

The injustice of the Conscription Act in allowing objectors to be forced into the Army, there to disobey orders on grounds of conscience and then to suffer severe and often brutal penalties, came to be recognized as a great mistake, and it is much to the credit of the Free Church Council that a juster and more humane policy was eventually adopted.

Extensive work was undertaken by the Council in connexion with the welfare of the troops. At the outbreak of the war, the Council urged all local Councils not to set up rival machinery but to co-operate with existing welfare organizations. By adopting this policy, the Free Churches prevented much duplication and rivalry, but it meant, inevitably, that a good deal of Free Church welfare and social work went unnoticed. In areas, however, where the need was acute, and where the existing organizations were in danger of being swamped, the Free Churches accomplished a prodigious amount of welfare work. All over the country Free Churches opened their schoolrooms and halls as centres of recreation and rest, and bands of Free Church volunteers cheerfully gave up their leisure hours to staff the canteens and rest rooms. Concerts and entertainments were organized, while on Sundays there were special soldiers' services with "sacred sing-songs". Many Free Church Councils started soldiers' clubs or institutes on their premises. One of the best examples was at Northampton, where the Free Church Council chartered a large building and converted it into a centre where canteen facilities, games rooms, writing and reading rooms were available. Many Free Church Councils organized permanent working parties which sent out regularly parcels, comforts, letters and greetings to all the troops whose homes were in that particular area. Many Free Church choirs gave special concerts for the troops and the wounded or in aid of Red Cross and Y.M.C.A. funds. Free Church ministers gladly, and in many cases without any material reward, laboured in camps and hospitals. In at least one area, the Free Church Council organized working parties to look after the gardens of men in the Forces, while another and original service which many local Councils organized was a scheme called "Snapshots from Home". Free Churchmen who were amateur photographers visited the homes of relatives of serving men and took photographs which were then despatched to the Front. The Holywell Free Church Council supplied every soldier in the town with a Bible, while the Long Eaton Council had a weekly chaplaincy rota for visitation of the homes of people who had lost men at the Front or whose menfolk had been wounded. Many Councils made themselves completely responsible for Belgian refugee families, notably at Blackpool and Penzance, while at Southport and Portsmouth the local Councils ran a most successful ambulance service for moving the wounded from the railway to hospital.

Another valuable contribution of the Free Church Council was a little magazine for servicemen, called *The Service Messenger*. This was supplied to troops at home and abroad, free of charge, and was really brought into being in response to appeals from chaplains at the Front. The magazine was deeply appreciated and evoked a continuous stream of letters of gratitude from chaplains and men. It claimed to be the only religious magazine published solely for the troops, and it was maintained entirely through voluntary contributions.

As we have seen, Free Church ministers had not been neglectful of national service. In 1918 there were over nine hundred commissioned chaplains with the Forces, and over two thousand others without commissions who were acting as chaplains in camps and hospitals. Many others were in full- or part-time service with such bodies as the Red Cross or Y.M.C.A. That such a considerable contribution was made by Free Church ministers was due to negotiations between Mr. Neville Chamberlain and the Free Church Council in February 1917, at a moment of crisis in the war. With the earnest efforts of every man needed, Mr. Chamberlain requested the Council to draw up a scheme with suggestions as to how ministers could best help the country in the emergency, and when the proposals were submitted to him, he approved them in their entirety. The proposals approved ministerial work in camps, hospitals, the Red Cross and other major welfare organizations, whether full- or part-time, as national service.

The 1919 Report of the Free Church Council informs us that in a single year over 1,200 items of war service work were performed by over 700 local Councils, and that altogether the Free Church Council was engaged in upwards of 200 different types of war service, often at the cost of great personal sacrifice. These figures, along with the cameo of examples we have looked at, may be left to tell their own tale in a situation in which Free Church manpower was seriously denuded by the increasing demands of the battlefield, and when all people were the victims of personal anxieties and fears. With a depleted staff at headquarters, and the same story in all the local Councils, with shortages and the countless difficulties which war brings on the civilian front, only the magnificent and unstinted service of Free Church women throughout the war years kept the whole organization moving sweetly and mightily when otherwise it must have disintegrated.

A great amount of time and money was directed towards the ideal of total abstinence during the war years. Huge posters and ambitious publicity schemes called on the British people to take the pledge of abstinence to help on the war effort. This campaign received a great fillip when the King himself announced his intention of abstaining from all intoxicating liquors during wartime. Two Sundays in April 1915 were held as King's Pledge Sundays, and special Pledge cards were circulated by the thousand. The campaign met with astonishing success, and within a comparatively short time over one million pledges were received. The case for total abstinence was cogently stated by John Clifford at the 1917 Free Church Council Assembly. Moving a resolution for the total prohibition of intoxicating liquor during the war, he pointed out that large quantities of valuable commodities such as barley, malt and sugar were being expended in the drink industry, and that precious tonnage space in the precarious business of importing was claimed by the same trade. Strong resolutions were sent to the Prime Minister, the Food Controller, and the Board of Trade, while in the gloomy days of 1917 when the submarines of the German fleet were threatening Britain with an acute food shortage, the Free Church Council again called for the total prohibition of the manufacture and sale of intoxicating liquor, and suggested that all spirits in bond should be commandeered for munition purposes.

The fact that severe restrictions both in the manufacture and sale of alcoholic liquor were imposed during the war years by the War Control Board was very largely due to the extensive and sustained campaigns of protest by the Free Church Council along with other bodies. In March 1918, Lloyd George, speaking to the Free Church Council, revealed that the amount of liquor consumed at the beginning of 1918 was one-third of the 1914 figure.

Despite the vast amount of work which the Free Church Councils did in connexion with specifically wartime problems, the normal work went on without interruption during wartime. Extensive evangelistic work went on, and mission vans rendered yeoman service, particularly in rural areas. Open-air services were held on a large scale, and many missions to the forces were undertaken, quite apart from cinema and theatre services. Although no large-scale missions took place in wartime, such as the great Simultaneous Missions, it is quite false to represent the evangelistic enterprise of the Council as in abeyance during the war. There were new opportunities presented by the exigency of wartime conditions, and these were eagerly accepted.

As might be expected, the war produced a deepening sense of unity amongst Free Churchmen, and this smoothed the way for the advent of the Federal Council in 1919. During the war years there was a big increase in the number of united meetings for intercession and devotional fellowship. Nor was this confined to the Free Churches. The rift between Anglicans and Free Churchmen began to narrow, and grievous and bitter wounds quickly showed signs of healing. Many Free Church Councils reported joint meetings of intercession with Anglicans, and in Hull, even the Roman Catholics joined in a common campaign against immorality and intemperance. At Harrogate in 1915, both Roman Catholics and Anglicans joined in a "Call to Prayer" Campaign organized by the Council. A new spirit of unity and service began to permeate the ranks of all types of Christians, and many of the old prejudices and divisions, whilst not disappearing, certainly began to lose a good deal of their sting. It is from the Great War that we begin to trace the growing improvement in the relations of Anglicans and Free Churchmen. It is tragic and regrettable that so often it takes a grave emergency or crisis to stimulate Christians to a unity of purpose and service, and to a vision of the things that really matter.

In times of comparative ease and well being, the attention of the churches has so frequently been fixed upon matters belonging to the perimeter and not the centre of the Kingdom of God, and yet we never seem to learn the lesson.

An interesting and effective experiment was undertaken by the Council in January 1915. The "Come to Church" campaign was one of the most ambitious efforts ever launched by the Council and ranked second only to the great Simultaneous Missions in the first decade of the century. The publicity which the campaign received calls for some comment. One original feature was the issue of millions of coloured stamps of postage size for use in correspondence either on the outside of the envelope or at the base of the letter. These stamps vividly advertised the effort to reach outsiders on two Sundays—January 24 and 31. The co-operation of the Press in spite of war news was quite remarkable, and the Free Church Council claimed that over fifty daily papers inserted articles for many weeks. An astonishing amount of literature flowed out of Memorial Hall in the shape of handbills, pamphlets, posters and invitation cards. It is estimated that over ten million invitations were sent out. Intensive house-to-house visitation preceded zero hour, and at Hull, every single house was visited by the Free Church Council at least twice, and many of them four times. On the two Campaign Sundays, many churches were full to overflowing, while large increases in congregations were reported everywhere. Although not a few people were received into Church membership as a result, and old contacts successfully renewed, the campaign did not seem to have any appreciable effect upon the twenty-seven million folk estimated to be beyond the influence of the churches. It is worth noting that over nine hundred and fifty Free Church Councils were actively engaged in this campaign.

The Annual Assemblies of the Council continued to meet during the war years, although the programmes were severely curtailed. The most interesting debate was in 1915 at Manchester upon the issue of pacifism. Alfred Garvie warned his hearers that Christianity was universal so that patriotism could not be exclusive, and that a spirit of Christian love and understanding should be sought in public sentiment and popular emotion. Dr. H. T. Hodgkin claimed that even so called "justifiable" wars were anti-Christian. He pointed out that Christ left Himself defenceless, that He refused to use weapons, and that His method of dealing with evil was by confronting it with good. In war, said Dr. Hodgkin, we are saying that Christ's method is out of date. He summoned the Council to eschew the method of militarism and to take Christ's path even if it led to a traitor's death. The Rev. Thomas Nightingale agreed that war was anti-Christian, but went on to take a quite different line. The war, he said, was supporting and advancing a great moral idea by opposing a despotic race which had tried to wipe out every landmark of public morality. Germany, said Thomas Nightingale, had no regard for sacred treaties which were the essential foundation of all human society in principle. At a great Free Church rally in the Free Trade Hall during the Council, both John Clifford and Arthur Henderson, M.P., supported participation in the war, but Mrs. Philip Snowden with tremendous courage delivered a scathing indictment of the churches and their leaders for their support of military action. Her pacifism evoked considerable and noisy protest from the body of the hall. The majority of Free Churchmen, and a vast majority it was, held no brief for either Mrs. Snowden's or Dr. Hodgkin's point of view. Free Churchmen felt, with Thomas Nightingale, that when the foundations of order and morality are grossly assaulted, then the duty of every man is to defend them vigorously.

Lloyd George's wooing of the Free Churches in his great speech in the previous November had been the decisive turning-point.

A final word should be said about the political situation. When the war commenced, the 1910 government was still in office with Mr. Asquith as Prime Minister of a Liberal Government with the Labour and Irish Nationalist parties really holding the balance. In 1915 the government was reconstituted as a coalition of all parties with Mr. Asquith as Premier and David Lloyd George as Minister of Munitions. In 1916, a further change came when Lloyd George took over from Asquith as Premier and introduced a special War Cabinet of Ministers without special departmental responsibilities so that they could devote themselves entirely to the war effort. Under the vigorous leadership of Lloyd George, Britain showed a greater unity of purpose than ever before in the war. A somewhat large section of the Liberals under Mr. Asquith, however, stood aloof from and gave only critical support to the new Coalition, and at the end of the war the Labour membersof the Cabinet withdrew, the Coalition thus becoming largely Conservative, although led by a Liberal. As soon as the war was over, a General Election was held on a wider franchise than ever before, for towards the end of the war, the Franchise Act had given the vote to women over thirty and to all men over twenty-one. The Coalition, largely Conservative, appealed to the country to support the men who had won the war, and they were returned with an overwhelming majority. The Labour Party came back with 62 seats; the Asquith Liberals were reduced to 26; the Irish Nationalist party was almost obliterated; and the Coalition Government was undisputed victor.

The Free Church Council took no side in this election but issued an interesting election manifesto calling for the immediate establishment of the League of Nations; the true partnership in industry between employers and employed; the complete emancipation of women; Health, Housing and Educational Reform; and ample and generous provision for the disabled soldiers, the widows and orphans. It was indeed a utopian manifesto at that time, but almost forty years later we salute it as a remarkably enlightened one.

On November 16, 1918, the Free Church Council summoned Free Churchmen to a Solemn Thanksgiving Service in the Royal Albert Hall. It was attended by King George V and Queen Mary. History was made that day, for it was the first time that a reigning monarch had ever attended a Free Church ceremony. A lot of water, indeed, had flowed under the bridge of ecclesiastical history since the stormy days of 1902.

Chapter 10

SOCIAL CONCERN

SINCE the first decade of the century the Free Church Council had been gravely disturbed by the growing indifference of the working classes to the Free Churches. Hugh Price Hughes, J. Scott Lidgett, J. E. Rattenbury, and J. B. Paton all affirmed the social redemptive mission of the Free Churches and tried many experiments through which that mission might be fulfilled. For example, in 1906, the Social Questions Committee of the Free Church Council, largely guided by Dr. Paton, put forward a Scheme of Social Reconstruction pleading for a number of necessary and urgent reforms. This scheme makes remarkable reading to-day. So much do we take for granted these reforms now that it is difficult for most of us to understand that fifty years ago men were pleading and toiling agonizingly for them.

In any history of social reform in the early years of this century the Free Churches deserve honourable mention, for they were among the first to recognize and plead the claims of the exploited working classes. The beginnings of major social reform in the measures promoted by the Liberal Government after 1906 were strongly and enthusiastically supported by Free Churchmen. Moreover, many of the great Labour pioneers came from Free Church backgrounds and received their early training as speakers in Free Church circles.[1] Many of these early leaders of

[1] For example, Arthur Henderson (1863–1935), a Wesleyan lay preacher; Keir Hardie (1856–1915), also a lay preacher; J. Ramsay Macdonald, a deeply religious man. These three were prominent among the founders of the British Labour movement.

the Labour cause were devout Christians who recognized that the Gospel of Jesus Christ was concerned with every aspect and department of human activity, and, that to confine it to one, was to produce a dangerous and unscriptural salvationism. One of the tragedies of our century is that as the Labour movement progressed, it tended to become an end in itself, and the gospel of Socialism, at any rate, very largely lost its religious inspiration and stimulus, and became in certain quarters a materialistic creed.

There is no doubt that within the Free Churches, and largely because of Free Church Council activity, there was an increasing desire to apply the Gospel in concrete terms to the great social problems. Social institutes were set up in various parts of the country and they accomplished invaluable work, particularly in the distressed areas. At Blackheath in Staffordshire, free meals were provided for children by the Free Church Council, and at Putney the Council organized a soup kitchen which catered faithfully for all the needy. At Pwllheli, where great numbers of navvies were engaged upon harbour work, the Free Church Council acquired a large site and provided temporary dwellings for the workers. Volunteer missioners worked amongst the men, who proved the more amenable and approachable after such obvious concern for their material welfare. And so, one could go on to multiply examples of the social labours of the Council in the early years of the century. The Birmingham National Council of 1906 expressed the determination of Free Churchmen to support Labour in its effort to secure better conditions for the poor and the distressed.

In 1908, the Chairman of the Labour Party, Mr. Arthur Henderson, appeared on the Council platform at Southport, and the earnest attention given to his statement of Labour ideals was perhaps indicative of the concern of

Free Churchmen at the continued and growing indifference of the working classes to the Free Churches. This Southport Assembly, however, will best be remembered for the magnificent defence of Socialism delivered by the Rev. J. Ernest Rattenbury. He defined Socialism as a great human movement with a passion for the masses worthy of the greatest religious zeal. He claimed that the churches should be one with Socialism in its abhorrence of modern conditions; in its view of individual life as more important than property; and in its effort to reconstruct society in terms at any rate nearer to the Kingdom of God than the prevailing ones. Socialism needs Christianity, said Rattenbury, and Christianity can use Socialism. He rightly condemned the vulgar and furious attacks which accused Socialism of immoral and atheistic foundations, as worthy only of a gutter press. It is difficult for us to realize the extreme vehemence of the attacks frequently levelled at Socialism in the first decade of the century. The word was equated, like the word "Bolshevist" to-day for many people, with revolution, lawlessness and the overthrow of all good and stable forces.[1]

Addresses on social problems continued to appear in the programme of the National Council, and in 1911 Mr. J. Ramsay Macdonald, M.P., the Labour leader, later to be Prime Minister, addressed the Council on the disturbing problem of industrial unrest. It was in this same year that the Insurance Bill, one of the greatest and most far-reaching pieces of legislation since the Reform Bill or the Repeal of the Corn Laws, passed smoothly through the Lords. The interplay between the Nonconformist conscience and Liberalism had not a little to do with the comparatively smooth beginning of a new social era.

[1] The present writer whilst serving with the British Army in Berlin, was profoundly shocked at the fear and intense hatred of the Bolshevists by the Germans. They were regarded as verminous outcasts scheming to overthrow all stable forces of security and usher in a reign of terror.

The Free Churches never gained any strong foothold within the Labour camp, however, despite the overtures made and the strong support of social reform in Parliament, and the close of the Great War found the Free Churches growing more and more alarmed at their inability to intervene effectively in the ferment between capital and labour. In 1919 the Free Church Council found it hard to accept that Nonconformity which had once been in the van of all reform, the champion of the underdog, must stand by and watch what promised to be, and indeed was, a major social revolution moving steadily ahead, largely divorced from religious motive and inspiration.

Speculation at this point is interesting but not very profitable. Could the Labour movement at the dawn of its life, numbering as it did many Christians within its ranks and a few at its helm, have been harnessed to the Free Churches and tempered by Christian guidance? Why did Labour appear reluctant to respond to the attempted courtship by the Free Churches? Overtures undoubtedly were made, and there was much sympathy for Labour within the Free Church Council and, indeed, one or two powerful spokesmen. Was Labour stubborn and independent or was the courtship insincere? It could not have been that there was no common ground for the facts clearly show that, given a little sympathy, goodwill and determination on both sides, there might well have been a real liaison. The fault lay with both sides. The connotation of the word "socialism" to which reference has already been made, and the emotional reaction it often evoked, was not sweet medicine to the middle-class people who, very largely, constituted the effective portion of the Free Churches. Again, the majority of Free Churchmen were Liberals, and convinced ones, and with the successful attack on the Lords' veto safely pressed home, they no doubt felt that the Liberal Government was well placed to do much good work, as indeed it did. On the Labour side, though there were a number of Christian leaders, it is a mistake to think of the Labour group even in those early years as a Christian entity, as some people seem to believe. It is certain that there was always a powerful section who desired to fight Labour's battle apart from any religious help or sympathy, and even those who might have accepted such help were not encouraged to ask for it when they were confronted with a good deal of suspicion and misunderstanding, coupled with a conservative love of *laisser-faire*. The Labour movement therefore had little alternative but to close its ranks and to turn in upon itself. Rightly or wrongly, Labour decided that if the Church was the ally of privilege and monopoly, then Labour would fight alone.

Since 1919 there has been little improvement in this particular situation. Whether we like it or not, the Free Churches are not the places where the needy, the depressed, the lowly and the shameful seek a home and shelter. We have only to look round the average Free Church to-day to discover the truth of it. How much this present unfortunate situation owes to those thousands of people, so frequently the critics of the Free Church Council, who in the name of a false spirituality found their faith a refuge from life instead of a weapon to shape and transform it, will never be fully known, but certainly much blame must be laid at their door. At least the Free Church Council could claim such prophets as Hugh Price Hughes, John Clifford, John Scott Lidgett, and others whose viewpoint history has surely vidicated. When the Church withdraws from the battle of the world and seeks to keep itself intact and untarnished, then both Church and the world are well on the way to losing their souls.

After 1919, none the less, the Free Church Council

continued to provide a platform for the prolonged and earnest debate between capital and labour. In 1921, for example, Lord Leverhulme put the case for capitalism, claiming that it had been responsible for a great advance in the material conditions of the nation for all ranks of society. The case for labour was powerfully set out by Mr. J. Lawson, M.P., who claimed that if unemployment was a permanent and necessary feature of a capitalist society, then it was a truly terrible thing for a great civilization. Some of his words moved his audience deeply:

> If Labour is wrong, then the Free Churches have misled us. For it has taught us that human life is sacred . . . that this is God's world . . . that mankind is one, whatever its race, colour or creed. It has taught us to take seriously the coming of that time when swords shall be beaten into ploughshares. No organization has contributed more to this task than the Free Churches.[1]

Dr. R. F. Horton, in a masterly address, attempted to reconcile the two points of view when he urged that capital should be held and administered for the good of the community, and that it should rest in private hands only so long as it served the general good. He appealed to both capital and labour to apply spiritual principles of mutual love and concern for each other's interests in commerce and industry.

In 1923 Mr. (later Sir) Angus Watson, the owner of a great business, speaking at the National Free Church Council in Bristol, took much the same view in an impressive address permeated by a humble, generous and co-operative spirit. He claimed that real success in business was measured by the happiness of employees and not by monetary gain. The ideal business, he said, provides at all points for the physical and moral well-being of every employee. It would have a profit-sharing scheme for every

[1] *Free Church Year Book 1921*, p. 83.

member, and it would impose a limit on dividends on invested capital. It would not pay an inactive capitalist more than a reasonable return on his investments, and it would be controlled by directors prepared to work at least as hard as any member of the staff. Labour and capital together, said Mr. Watson, are needed for true progress, for production is not the fruit of labour only. Every man, whatever his position, should contribute his best, and approach business from the standpoint of service and not profit.

Mr. C. J. G. Ammon, J.P., L.C.C., M.P. (later Lord Ammon), a Trades Union worker, said that there were two opposing civilizations in the community, one fearful of the undermining of their security and luxury, the other resentful that the wealth of others was the product of their labour. Between these two sections was perpetual antagonism and ill will. Mr. Ammon claimed that the internal management of each industry should be in the hands of the workers, and that the object of the concern should be the welfare of the community and not the profit of particular individuals. He admitted that the problem of control was an extremely difficult one and he could see no solution short of a drastic change in the whole industrial system bringing with it an approach to the economic equality of all classes.

These two debates have been selected because they were two of the outstanding ones. There were, of course, many others, and the national assemblies repeatedly passed resolutions voicing the distress and concern of Free Churchmen at the appalling suffering and deterioration resulting from unemployment. These resolutions urged the government to take all steps to relieve a dreadful situation by undertaking public works and by extending such a policy as far as was humanly possible. Moreover, the Council repeatedly called on the Free Churches to throw open their halls and schoolrooms to shelter and befriend the distressed and the homeless.

On two occasions the Prime Minister, the Rt. Hon. J. Ramsay Macdonald, appeared on the Council platform, at Brighton in 1924, and in London in 1929. On both occasions he attracted huge gatherings and was accorded a royal welcome, and both his addresses were searching and challenging inquiries into the grave social problems of a pleasure-loving age.

The Free Church Council in all this troublous time did its best to bring goodwill into the relationships on both sides of the industrial problem, and it constantly summoned Free Churchmen to see Christ in all faces and in every social group, and to be conscious of the Spirit and purpose of Christ in shop, office and factory. In 1926, for example, the Council made an actual appeal to the associations of owners and workers in the mining industry to avert an industrial crisis and to settle their bitter disputes by conciliation and goodwill, but in a situation fraught with tension and passion the appeal went unheeded, and within a few weeks the turmoil gave birth to the famous General Strike of 1926, with its appalling results.

The Free Church Council never seemed to give up hope of being able to influence for good the social problems of these tense years between the two world wars. In the thirties, the Council continued its ministrations to the distressed, and many local Councils engaged in extensive relief work, providing recreation centres to arrest the awful deadening of morale. The Council was constantly in touch with the National Council of Social Service, and no effort was spared to keep abreast of this vast and terrible feature of English life.

At last there came a moment when an opportunity to strike a real blow seemed to present itself. In 1933, Mr.

Lloyd George addressed the National Free Church Council at Sheffield. In the City Hall, packed to the doors, Lloyd George was at his best. He expressed great concern at the problem of growing unemployment, and he warned his vast audience that everything might depend upon the speedy action of the Christian churches. Soon afterwards, the Free Church Council arranged a conference between Mr. Lloyd George and certain Free Church leaders for an exchange of opinion upon the possibilities of action by the churches in relation to unemployment and international peace. All denominations sent representatives to this conference, and the outcome was that, after Mr. Lloyd George had made certain recommendations, a small committee was set up to consult with the Free Church Council Executive. The result of these deliberations was that in July 1935 a Convention on Peace and Unemployment was held in the Central Hall, Westminster. Every member of the Council Executive was invited to attend, and the Executive urged the local Councils to co-operate. This Convention approved a manifesto, "A Call to Action", which was signed by Mr. Lloyd George, a number of Free Church leaders, and some other distinguished people, appealing to all good citizens, irrespective of party, class or profession, to decide what action they would require from the new Parliament, when elected,[1] on the issues in particular of International Peace and National Unemployment. The conference also resulted in the nation wide organization of the Council of Action for Peace and Reconstruction, as the movement became known. Local Councils and Committees were formed all over the country in the parliamentary constituencies, and these were designed to act in harmony with a National Council directing policy.[2] The movement, in other words, was not

[1] Reference to the General Election of November, 1935.

[2] Dr. S. M. Berry told me in an interview that it was never the intention of the Free Church signatories of the Manifesto that independent candidates

unlike the Free Church Council organization in structure.

When the National Council of Action was formed, several leading Free Churchmen were invited to serve upon it. Mr. Angus Watson became the Chairman of the Executive; Dr. Scott Lidgett, vice-Chairman, and Mr. R. Wilson Black, J.P., the Treasurer. The Council also promoted a number of vigorous Area Conventions to stir up the electorate on the issues of Peace and Unemployment. At these conventions many prominent Free Churchmen, including some of the leaders of the Free Church Council, addressed public meetings in support of the new movement. Dr. Scott Lidgett, Mr. Angus Watson, the Rev. J. Ivory Cripps, Dr. F. W. Norwood, the Rev. F. C. Spurr, the Rev. S. W. Hughes, the Rev. Dr. S. M. Berry, the Rev. Dr. Charles Brown, the Rev. Dr. J. D. Jones were among the Free Churchmen who rallied to the side of the Council of Action.

There was, however, considerable opposition to the new movement from many Free Churchmen, and to the association of Free Church Council leaders with it. However, in early July, the Free Church Council Executive, in view of the urgency of the problems of peace and unemployment, advised local Free Church Councils to associate with the local Councils of Action always provided that:

(*a*) the latter's programme and questionnaire to Parliamentary candidates conformed with the resolutions of the Annual Assemblies of the Free Church Council;

(*b*) the movement kept clear of party politics or the policy of any particular statesman (an obvious reference to Mr. Lloyd George);

(*c*) care was taken to unite and not divide the local Free Church Councils.

should be promoted. The sole idea was to secure that, in the next Parliament, there would be a great body of members of all parties pressing for more vigorous and competent action with regard to the great problems of International Peace and Unemployment.

Thus the support of the new movement by the Free Church Council was only conditional, and the conditions clearly absolved the Free Church Council from any intention of promoting a new political party.

Dr. J. C. Carlile, the Editor of the *Baptist Times*, was very critical of the Free Church Council in this matter, and he brought forward a serious allegation without any real evidence:

> The Free Churches . . . should not take party action. . . . Many years ago I resigned from the Free Church Council on that ground. Only once in thirty years have I been upon a Council platform. That body long ago should have been an organic part of the Federal Council; it would have been but for party politics. . . .[1]

Such groundless criticism should not delay us long, for the continued existence of the Free Church Council, as we shall see, came about because the movement was meeting a need which the Federal Council did not profess to meet. None the less, Dr. Carlile was a spokesman for those who were inclined to be conservative in their view of what action the Free Churches might legitimately take in the secular sphere, and, one suspects, conservative in politics also.

Dr. M. E. Aubrey, Secretary of the Baptist Union, resigned his position on the Executive of the Free Church Council in protest against its policy in support of the Council of Action, and a vigorous correspondence developed in the columns of the *Baptist Times*, with Dr. Aubrey on one side with his supporters, among them of course the Editor, and Dr. Charles Brown, Mr. Wilson Black, and Dr. S. W. Hughes and their sympathizers on the other.

Dr. Aubrey resigned because he objected to a "quasi-

[1] *Baptist Times*, July 4, 1935.

representative body like the Free Church Council" lending its influence to a document and a movement which seemed purely partisan. Unfortunately, as his critics were not slow to point out, he resigned before the Free Church Council had considered the matter. Dr. Aubrey's defence was that the original manifesto bore the signature of the president, the two secretaries and the two treasurers of the Free Church Council, and was delivered to him by the secretary from the offices of the Free Church Council. Dr. S. W. Hughes, however, made it perfectly clear that the signatures carried only individual significance, and, in any event, as S. W. Hughes went on to suggest, the action of Dr. Aubrey was inconsistent because the signatures of a number of members of the Federal Council were also on the manifesto, including that of the Moderator, the Rev. Dr. S. M. Berry, but Dr. Aubrey had not been provoked thereby to resign his membership of the Federal Council.

Much of the opposition to the Free Church Council's support of the Council of Action was due to the prominence of the notorious figure of Mr. Lloyd George, who was very much of a stormy petrel in the political world, and it is true to say that there had been a widespread loss of faith in him in the years which followed the first World War. Many people suspected that the Council of Action might be a piece of political trickery designed to enable Lloyd George to ride victoriously back to power.

The movement seems to have been the suggestion of Mr. Lloyd George, some time after his address to the Free Church Council in 1933, when he spoke of the urgent need to do something drastic about the problems of Peace and Unemployment. Mr. Wilson Black said that Lloyd George was pressed to help the Free Church Council in this connexion, and that it was made clear to him from the outset that any proposed action would have to be kept clear of party politics. The present writer interviewed two of the leaders of the Council of Action—two eminent Free Churchmen, the Rev. Dr. Sidney M. Berry and the Rev. Dr. S. W. Hughes. Both agreed that the aims of the Council of Action were wholly commendable. They constituted a genuine attempt to :

> stir the awful stagnant waters of that time,[1]

and to stimulate the government to take some quick and radical action.

Both Dr. Berry and Dr. Hughes did not regret the stand they had taken, because they considered that at such a time, any measures which would have jolted the government and stirred up action were wholly justified. They both felt that the full gravity and extreme urgency of the situation had not been appreciated by the government, and that a startling innovation like the Council of Action might have succeeded where ordinary representations had failed. So far so good, it would seem, but Mr. Lloyd George, having secured much influential support from the Free Churches, seems to have revealed intentions of developing the movement beyond the limits agreed. It may have been that he began to see that the Council of Action could easily become a way back to political power for himself; it may be, of course, that he had intended something like that from the outset and that to use a semireligious veneer was a useful cloak. In the recent biography of Mr. Lloyd George by Thomas Jones, C.H., who had very close contact with his fellow countryman, one discovers this extremely interesting observation:

> The Council of Action, founded in the summer of 1935, was a fresh attempt by Lloyd George to get his hands on the

[1] Dr. Berry's words to the present writer in an interview on November 7, 1950, at the Memorial Hall.

> levers of power at the next election by means of an organization under his own control.[1]

This, no doubt, explains why the original Free Church supporters of the movement became increasingly cautious and began to withdraw, with the result that, although the Council of Action did for a time stir the government,[2] it never really established itself as a vital force, and it gradually disappeared. The mode of its disappearance was strange. Both Dr. Berry and Dr. Hughes confessed that it would be difficult to say exactly how and when the movement ended. Although Thomas Jones refers to it as late as 1939, it seems that it gradually declined and, generally speaking, it was more or less eclipsed by the increasing threat of Nazism and Fascism. Thus ended, unlamented and unsung, one of the most intriguing minor episodes of British public life in the tense and perplexing years between the two World Wars.

It is fairly clear that the motives of the Free Church Council Executive in co-operating with the Council of Action were, to say the least, largely disinterested and certainly unpolitical. As Dr. Berry put it, the idea was not to initiate an independent party or to press the claims of a single party, or the claims of a particular statesman, but to secure a body of men drawn from all parties who would be vigorous and conscientious in their treatment of the vital problems of peace and unemployment. By such action, the Free Church Council helped to relieve the persistent and hopeless feeling of frustration experienced by many people in face of the distress and uncertainty in the home country and abroad. It was something they could set their hands to, and it is not surprising when we remember those regrettable days, that they felt that

[1] See Thomas Jones, C.H., *Lloyd George*, 1951, O.U.P., p. 243.

[2] Dr. Berry, for example, was summoned to Lord Simon and closely interrogated.

almost any action was better than inaction, indifference and despair.

The Free Church Council never gave up hope of being able to bring a helpful and a Christian influence to bear upon the social problems of the day. In the years between the wars not a great deal was accomplished, but that was by no means due solely to the inadequacy of the Council's endeavours, and it can at least be said that the Council never stopped trying and that it always bore the burden of distress and need upon its conscience and within its heart. It was said, after all, of a great mountaineer, who did not reach his goal, that he died climbing. It is a not inglorious epitaph.

Chapter 11

THE LAMBETH CONVERSATIONS

THE first World War brought forward the whole problem of Church reunion. Co-operation on the battlefield between chaplains and men of all churches and denominations, and the deep experience of comradeship which war fosters, produced among many Christians a sense of disquiet and even shame, and a growing desire for the healing of the divisions of Christendom. The war also fostered a certain democratic trend in human affairs. Men began to look with longing and hope to the League of Nations, which was the embodiment on the grand scale of the impulse towards co-operation and unity which was felt by millions of hearts. Many considered that what was being attempted on the political scale might profitably be introduced into the religious sphere. The isolation and independence which had enabled the churches in all the warring nations to stand solidly behind political leaders and to bless their own national war aims was felt to be something of an offence and a disgrace. God could hardly answer all the prayers of His children!

It was to a distracted world groping for solidarity and unity then, that the Lambeth Conference of Anglican Bishops in 1920 directed the famous document "An Appeal to All Christian People".

The appeal was a lofty and memorable utterance, and it ushered in a new stage in the relations between Anglicans and Free Churchmen. It pointed men to the vision and goal of a reunited Catholic Church based on the wholehearted acceptance of Holy Scripture, the Creeds, the Sacraments of Baptism and Holy Communion, and a Ministry possessing the call of the Spirit, and the authority of the whole body of Christ. The appeal evoked a friendly and sympathetic response from the Free Churches, and a Joint Committee of the Federal Council and the Free Church Council was set up to prepare a detailed reply, the aim being not to answer, accept or reject the proposals but to set forth the general principles in the light of which the Free Churches might consider them. This committee, chaired by Dr. W. B. Selbie and convened by Dr. Carnegie Simpson, published in March 1921 a statement known as "The Free Churches and the Lambeth Appeal",[1] which was subsequently endorsed by the Free Church denominations. The statement really centred upon three important elements in the Lambeth proposals. Were the Anglicans prepared to recognize non-episcopal communions as corporate parts of the Church of Christ, and their ministries as real ministries? Would Free Church ministries have to be "made" ministries in the Church of Christ according to the Anglican Ordinal? Would the civil power have any authority over the spiritual affairs of the Church?

This Free Church statement created widespread interest, and as a result the Archbishop of Canterbury, Dr. Davidson, suggested that the Free Churches might enter into fraternal conference with delegates from the Church of England. Thus there began an important and historic series of meetings at Lambeth, the like of which had not been seen since the abortive Savoy Conference of 1661. These discussions were between officially authorized representatives, so that on the Free Church side the negotiations were conducted henceforward by the Federal Council, which was thus confronted very early in its career with a most formidable task.

[1] G. K. A. Bell, *Documents on Christian Unity* (1920–1924), 1924, p. 120.

For some four years the conversations at Lambeth were sustained, and a number of important points emerged. In July 1923 there came from the Anglican side a declaration which Dr. Carnegie Simpson described as

> the most notable thing which Lambeth has said to any non-episcopal church since the time of, say, Bancroft or Laud.[1]

Dr. Carnegie Simpson tells how the Free Church delegates actually asked the Anglicans to reconsider the statement carefully in view of the fact that the Free Churches would make the greatest use of it. The Anglican statement recognized Free Church ministries to which authority had been given by the churches concerned, as real ministries of Christ's Word and Sacraments in the Universal Church. It was a statement presented personally by Dr. Lang and endorsed by all the members of the episcopal bench who were members of the Anglican delegation.

The statement was of course one which inspired high hopes in many Free Church hearts, but events were to prove that what the Church of England had given with one hand, it intended to take away with the other. The Federal Council quickly drew the natural conclusion. If Free Church ministries were conceded as real ministries of Christ's Word and Sacraments in the Universal Church, how could the Church of England demand that such ministers should be ordained to that identical ministry? In reply, the Anglicans claimed that no mere intention, however sincere, to preach the Word and administer the Sacraments was sufficient without any further examination, and because certain ministries were admitted as real ones, it did not necessarily mean that they were in themselves complete:

[1] P. Carnegie Simpson, *Recollections*, 1943, p. 78. cf. F. A. Iremonger, *William Temple*, pp. 457–458.

> Spiritual efficacy is one thing, due authority is another. The latter is not involved in the former.[2]

Episcopal ordination, said the Anglicans, was not merely desirable. It was something which had always been provided—no less than an actual token of the guidance of the Church by the Holy Spirit. It was pointed out that the Free Church delegates had tentatively agreed upon episcopal ordination for the order and life of a future, united Church, and that objections were only directed against the proposal that *existing* Free Church ministries should receive such authority. The problem was then a temporary one in a transitional period, and the Anglicans therefore considered and proposed a modification, namely Ordination *sub conditione*, or an Act of Episcopal Ordination according the the Ordinal of the Church of England, but conditioned by some such words as "If thou art not already ordained". The person ordained would then be simply acknowledging the existence of a doubt in the mind of the ordaining authority without admitting its validity himself. This was a sincere and genuine attempt by the Anglican delegates to find a way through the impasse, but the Federal Council would have nothing to do with any kind of an ordination and suggested that the only possible way forward seemed to be in terms of a "commission" which would be binding upon all, and would be, unambiguously, not an ordination.

There for the time being the matter rested, and the conversations were suspended. Some twenty or so meetings had been held over the course of four years, and to many it seemed that no really tangible result had been achieved. Yet the discussions had been carried on for a much longer period, and in a more lofty and Christian spirit, than in any previous meetings between Anglicans and Free Churchmen. Complete estrangement and separation had

[2] G. K. A. Bell, *Documents on Christian Unity* (2nd Series), 1930, p. 79.

been overcome, and a real measure of sympathy and goodwill—the essential pre-requisites of any lasting union—had been firmly established. The negotiations throughout had not aimed at actual reunion but were intended to remove misapprehension and to explore the main problems in an endeavour to discover possible lines of progress. Viewed thus, there can be little doubt that much was accomplished. The crucial issue turned out to be the ministry, as was only to be expected, and considerable divergence appeared at that point, but it should not be forgotten that a large area of agreement appeared in relation to the fundamental verities of the faith, and it was accepted that any polity must make adequate room for the voice of the presbytery and the congregation.

The Lambeth conversations were by no means approved by everybody. There was opposition on the Anglican side, and it was only to be expected that the Anglo-Catholics would view with suspicion and hostility any kind of a *rapprochement* with bodies they considered irregular. On the Free Church side, many viewed the activities of the Joint Conference at Lambeth with the gravest misgivings, and the correspondence which developed in the columns of the *British Weekly* was stormy and even discourteous. The strife was keenest in the "Independent" churches, and particularly the Baptists. A number of associations rejected the Report of the Joint Conference in 1922, and Dr. Henry Townsend went so far as to say that many Baptist churches considered that the pass was being sold behind their backs by the association of Dr. Shakespeare's name with the proposals. Many felt that Shakespeare's zeal for reunion might split the denomination from top to bottom. Dr. T. R. Glover was perhaps the most frequent opponent of the Lambeth conversations, and his letters in the daily press and the *British Weekly* displayed a sustained and penetrating invective. Deploring studied ambiguity, he wrote in the *Daily News*:

> If reunion depends on artificial fog, I for one am for daylight, for straight thinking and straight speech.[1]

Of the recognition of Free Church ministries, he wrote:

> It is difficult to write without irony of that tragic admission and its instant retraction. But logic and Lambeth do not hang together. . . .[2]

Grave concern was expressed in many areas of Congregationalism as well but, none the less, it is true to say that the majority of Free Churchmen did not display the same distrust of the Federal Council representatives on the Joint Conference as had Dr. Glover and Dr. Townsend. They came to realize that the treasured principles of the Evangelical Free Churches were in safe and able hands, and one has only to recall a few of the names of those who represented the Federal Council in the negotiations to appreciate their confidence: J. D. Jones, W. B. Selbie, A. S. Peake, Carnegie Simpson, R. C. Gillie, J. Scott Lidgett, A. E. Garvie, Charles Brown, W. T. Davison and J. H. Shakespeare.

There is no doubt that the Federal Council proved its worth. It was only in its infancy when it was summoned to face this major test of its efficiency and ability. The Lambeth conversations, it may be fairly claimed, established the Federal Council in the forefront of Free Church affairs, and won for it a respect and support which otherwise it might not have attained for another decade or more. The resolutions of the various denominations in 1926 showed that the Federal Council in its discharge of a most difficult task, and in its wise representation and

[1] *Daily News*, December 15, 1923.
[2] *ibid.*, April 5, 1924.

defence of Free Church principles, had won wide appreciation and approval. Dr. Henry Townsend, reviewing the matter more dispassionately over twenty years later, graciously admitted that the Federal Council had accomplished more than was generally conceded, in the matter of transforming the relations between Anglicans and Free Churchmen. It is refreshing to find support for the Federal Council in the columns of the *Baptist Times* during the period of denominational strife over Lambeth, when the editor could describe the negotiations as a great triumph for the policy of the Council.

No tribute to the Federal Council would be complete without coupling with it the name of Dr. Carnegie Simpson. His leadership can only be described as outstanding, and one of the most significant tributes came from one who had crossed swords with him on many an occasion, namely Henry Townsend:

> . . . Carnegie Simpson's leadership of Free Church discussions and negotiations with the Anglican leaders changed the religious atmosphere of the time and deserves honourable recognition.[1]

Carnegie Simpson proved himself to be an accomplished Free Church statesman. He won the widest respect and affection from opponents and colleagues alike. A skilled debater, not always easy in conference, he gained the firm friendship of both archbishops.

Why did the conversations not achieve more? On both sides there is little doubt that the leaders were far in advance of the rank and file of their followers. Secondly, as the Federal Council repeatedly emphasized, reunion discussions would always lack an essential element if they were not accompanied by practical and unmistakable acts of unity. This was and is the only way to make the vision

[1] H. Townsend, *The Claims of the Free Churches*, 1949, p. 313.

real to ordinary church members. It must in fairness be recognized that there were serious objections of principle on the Anglican side, and the two concessions[1] appended to the Lambeth Appeal were quite inadequate from the Free Church point of view. Thirdly, the recognition by the Church of England of Free Church ministries, and the immediate qualification which largely nullified it, really blocked all possibility of progress. Not only did Free Churchmen fail to understand the qualification but *The Times*, speaking for informed public opinion, wrote:

> The Free Church conclusion that this statement removes any necessity for the reordination of such ministers, even sub conditione, seems to the ordinary observer one that is obvious and natural and even irresistible.[2]

At the Lambeth Conference of 1930, only a slight reference was made to the discussions with the Free Churches, much to the disappointment of many Free Churchmen. Subsequently, the chairman of the Committee of Unity at Lambeth, Archbishop Temple, offered to publish a full apology, but this was wisely and graciously refused by Dr. Carnegie Simpson. In March 1931, however, the Archbishop of Canterbury formally invited the Federal Council to resume reunion conversations, and in September 1931 the Federal Council appointed new representatives on the understanding that the agreed results of the previous discussions should provide the basis for the new negotiations, and that a more practical policy with regard to acts of unity should be adopted.

[1] These provided for (*a*) occasional authorization by the Bishops to non-episcopal ministers to preach in Anglican churches provided they were working towards the Lambeth ideal of Reunion. (*b*) The Bishops would not question the action of any Bishop or priest who admitted baptized but not confirmed members of non-episcopal congregations to Communion provided those traditions were concerned in the Reunion talks, during the years between the start and completion of a scheme of union.

[2] *The Times*, September 25, 1925, article on "Progress in Reunion".

At the beginning of 1932 Convocation suggested that subject to the individual discretion of the bishops, Free Churchmen might be admitted to Holy Communion if they were unable to reach a church of their own order; if they were in a school or college where no Free Church service was held; or if they were present at some united conference or function. These concessions were regarded by some Free Churchmen as insults, and some urged the Federal Council to protest, but Dr. Hugh Martin proved to be a restraining force when he declared that to attack the bishops was hardly a fitting response to concessions which only a few years earlier would never have been considered at all. It was at least a step in the right direction, although, as Dr. Carnegie Simpson said, the qualification for a communicant was surely spiritual and had nothing to do with either the mileage to the next Presbyterian Church or the agenda of a conference!

When the Joint Conference reassembled after the Lambeth Conference of 1930, various courses were open to it. It might have attempted a more precise definition of principles formerly agreed upon, or it might have concentrated upon the question at issue when the talks were suspended in 1925, namely, the difficulties connected with the transition from separation. Neither of these courses was adopted as such. Instead, it was recognized that the chief obstacle to progress was the general indifference to and suspicion of projects of union among Christians at large, due to the anxiety lest valued elements in each particular system might be obscured or lost in union. The Joint Conference therefore decided not to wait for exact agreement upon principles but to concentrate on depicting a Church united in work and worship but with the valuable parts of each "separate" body preserved. It was felt that all reunion discussions would break down until men saw clearly the vision of what a united Church might be.

The result was a memorandum known as *A Sketch of a United Church.*

> People will not attempt a difficult crossing until they are persuaded that it is desirable to be on the other side.[1]

This was a very notable document, although perhaps a little too technical and detailed to arouse much popular interest. It endeavoured to work out in concrete terms what was involved in trying to combine the episcopal, presbyteral and congregational systems of church government, and it was based on the sincere conviction that in all those forms there were elements essential to the well-being of the Church and to the true nature of catholicity. As such, of course, it represented a real growth of understanding and unity among the leaders of the churches. It was a genuine effort to take a real step forward towards a "working hypothesis" which might kindle inspiration and enthusiasm for a great advance by the rank and file of Christians. It was also in part, as Dr. Hugh Martin suggested, the outcome of an interesting approximation to one another on the part of several traditions. The Church of England, for example, had deliberately been giving more authority to its laity, both centrally and in the parish. Presbyterians were leaning towards the idea of greater authority vested in the congregation, while Baptists and Congregationalists were moving slowly towards a modified connexionalism in the appointments of Area Superintendents and Moderators. The Federal Council received the document appreciatively and commended it to the earnest examination of the denominations as a basis for fruitful discussion and possible experiment.

Three years later, in January 1938, the Federal Council received from the Joint Conference another important document, known as "An Outline of a Reunion Scheme",

[1] *A Sketch of a United Church*, 1935, p. 6.

which set forth the kind of church in which British Christians might unite without loss of their distinctive treasures. Behind the "Outline", which incorporated within it the substance of the "Sketch", there was a draft prepared by the research group of the "Friends of Reunion", and it was originally drawn up by Dr. Hugh Martin. This draft was never published and never existed except in typed form, but it was submitted to the Joint Conference, and was closely followed in the official "Outline".[1]

The "Friends of Reunion" were formed in 1933, and they took over the name of a local group which had been functioning in the Birmingham area since 1931. The Friends were an unofficial body whose aim was to provide a popular movement to foster and develop the spirit and practice of unity among Christians of all traditions. Groups were formed all over the country to support united action and to make a wider public aware of the significance and importance of the Lambeth conversations.

The outbreak of war in 1939 and the indefinite postponement of the Lambeth Conference due in 1940, coupled with the negotiations for uniting the Federal Council with the Free Church Council, really brought to a standstill the conversations between the Church of England and the Free Churches, although in September 1941 the Federal Council published a statement based on the findings of the denominations. This document summarized the standpoint of the Free Churches with regard to reunion. Whilst agreeing that the conversations should go on, it was pointed out that many Free Churchmen believed that outward uniformity was not necessary to exhibit spiritual unity, and that, in any case, there were a number of serious differences not yet adequately reconciled.

[1] I am indebted to correspondence from Dr. Hugh Martin for this interesting information.

It seemed that the long and careful endeavours of twenty years had achieved little positive progress towards actual organic reunion, but at any rate much dead wood had been cleared away, the main problems were boldly revealed, and a new spirit of sympathy and fellowship had developed which augured well for the future.

The Federal Council, despite its mere twenty years of existence, had won wide respect and confidence, not only in Free Church circles but in Anglican ones also. The prominent part, thrust upon it by the Lambeth conversations, demanded responsible and skilled handling. The efficiency, dignity and discretion with which the Federal Council discharged a most involved task deserves the widest recognition and gratitude of all Free Churchmen. Nothing like its task had been attempted for some two hundred and sixty years. Considerable barriers of suspicion and prejudice blocked the way forward, yet, under God, it helped to transform the religious climate of our land, and usher in a new age of Christian fellowship and charity.

Chapter 12

SEARCH FOR PEACE

THE first World War came as a tremendous shock to the Free Churches. The easy optimism of the early years of the twentieth century was rudely shattered, and the measure of Free Church support for the League of Nations at the close of the war and in the years that followed was an indication of the determination to avoid, almost at any cost, a repetition of such a tragedy. Both the Federal and the Free Church Councils were strong and definite in their support of the League, and throughout the uneasy years of peace between the two wars they never entirely gave up hope that the nations of the world would eschew the arbitration of the sword, and would learn to settle their problems by means of the new instrument for peaceful co-operation which the Peace Treaty after the Great War had set up.

The Free Church Council, by reason of the fact that it was both a national and a local organization, naturally became the chief rallying point of Free Church support for the League, and a vast amount of practical work was accomplished. Peace meetings and rallies were a prominent feature of these uneasy years; millions of pamphlets were distributed by the local Councils; and every conceivable effort was made to stimulate public opinion in favour of making the League a practicable answer to international problems. For example, in 1922 alone, over five hundred Free Church Councils staged demonstrations in support of the League, and subsequently the plebiscite known as the Peace Ballot, initiated and organized by the League of Nations' Union, was widely canvassed and commended by hundreds of local Councils. In 1924, Viscount Cecil of Chelwood, addressing the National Free Church Council, could say:

> The League of Nations owes much to the Free Churches in this country, perhaps more than to any other Christian denomination. They have recognized the religious appeal of the League and have done their best to bring it home to the people.[1]

The Free Church Council repeatedly urged every Free Churchman to join the League of Nations' Union, and every congregation to ally itself with the World Alliance for International Friendship.

With this unequivocal support of the League there went a vigorous championing of the policy of disarmament. The annual assemblies of the Council passed resolutions in favour of disarmament almost every time they met, and when eventually the first World Disarmament Conference came together at Geneva in 1932 it was hailed with acclamation by the Council, and even the "Wayside Pulpit" took a hand and produced a special poster bearing the words, "Friendships are better than battleships".

The part played by the Federal Council was necessarily a good deal smaller because it was a national organization composed of official representatives who were, in the nature of the case, more cautious and less vociferous than their brethren of the popular and unofficial voice on the Free Church Council. None the less, the Federal Council was strong in its support of the League of Nations' Union and the World Alliance for International Friendship. For example, in 1931, the Federal Council sent out a statement to all Free Church congregations, urging them to make use of the existing organizations for the promotion of

[1] *Free Church Year Book 1924*, p. 23.

peace, and especially those of international significance. The Federal Council was also solidly in favour of world disarmament, and in 1933 expressed its satisfaction that the government

> are willing to go to the limit of sacrifice and to the edge of risk, because we are so convinced that it is only by international co-operation for the reduction of armaments that we can hope to secure . . . the peace of the world.

Midway through the 'thirties, however, the idealistic dreams of the Free Churches received a rude shock. It really began in 1933, when Hitler swept aside the Weimar Constitution, and ruthlessly began to crush all opposition to his new regime. Liberals and Jews were hounded and persecuted and the new regime established itself in a reign of terror. In 1934, on the death of the old president, Marshal Hindenburg, Hitler added the title of president to that of chancellor, and his authority was supreme. Maintaining that other powers had failed to disarm, Hitler immediately set about creating a powerful German Army and Air Force. In 1935, on the pretext that Germany could not be expected to leave her Rhine frontier exposed, Hitler marched his troops into the Rhineland. German rearmament continued at an alarming speed, and in 1938 Hitler's talons fastened upon Austria. The Sudetenland and Czechoslovakia were the next victims, and in 1939, on Germany's invasion of Poland and the famous Danzig corridor, the gauntlet which had been flung down so often and so brazenly, was finally accepted by the western democracies.

That, in brief, is the background of the last fateful years of our story in this chapter. It is not surprising that the Free Churches were shocked. The problem of how the League was to enforce its authority against a military aggressor had been, to all practical purposes, ignored. The cry had been for general disarmament. From 1933 and

1934 onwards, as the situation in Europe began to boil up, a significant change began to appear in Free Church opinion. Would the League endeavour to curb German aggression—if so, how? If not, what would Germany do?—where would she stop?

In 1935 Dr. F. W. Norwood's presidential address to the Free Church Council examined the problem. It was called, "The Free Churches and the Military State". It created much interest, but it was a perplexing mixture. Dr. Norwood asserted that the duty of the churches was a complete repudiation of war, but he proceeded to uphold the right of self-defence. He suggested an international tribunal which could impose economic restrictions upon recalcitrant aggressors, and in the last resort, an international air force which could be directed against aggressor armies and fleets. We will support, said Dr. Norwood, every effort towards the pacification of the world, even the putting of armed force behind a just and equal law, but we will not agree to the riveting of the war system upon us, or to the amassing of armaments as an attempted guarantee of security. This seems to be inconsistent.

Firstly, if the churches were to repudiate war completely, how could they support the promotion of a centralized armed force to resist aggression? and, secondly, if the Free Churches accepted that in certain circumstances a just law might have to be backed by some kind of force, then surely rearmament was necessary to equip the force in question and to keep it sufficiently strong to deter an aggressor. It would not be much use organizing the force after aggression had taken place. The confusion in Dr. Norwood's suggestion, however, was not confined to himself or indeed to the Free Churches. History has since revealed that nowhere was there a greater refusal to face facts than in Whitehall itself. All Free Churchmen, generally speaking, were with Dr. Norwood in the distinction he drew between war as such and the use of force to maintain peace, but the manufacture of armaments was clearly as necessary to the latter as the former, unless the scheme was to defeat its own avowed object.

Dr. Norwood's address, however, startled doctrinaire pacifists by its contemplation of force under certain defined conditions, and thereafter, in the Free Church Council debates, and to a lesser degree in the Federal Council's endeavour to discover a united peace policy for the churches, the issue of pacifism became prominent. In each case the pacifist pressure upon the Free Churches to declare that they would have no lot or part in any kind of force was decisively rejected. Dr. Norwood himself interpreted the general feeling of Free Churchmen in these tense years when he said that the cause of peace could not possibly be advanced if it were known for certain that the British nation would never fight again under any circumstances at all.

As Hitler, emboldened by the unqualified success of his programme of aggression thus far, became more ambitious, considerable feeling against him and his partner in crime, Mussolini, developed in Free Church circles, and it became increasingly recognized on all sides, and particularly in the debates in the Free Church Council, that the most sincere negotiations and overtures of goodwill had little chance of success with powers which could cheerfully, and at will, repudiate the most solemn obligations.

None the less, although the majority of Free Churchmen from 1935 onwards would probably have seriously considered some measure of rearmament—and in fact many accepted the inevitability of it in their own minds—they felt that such convictions should not be expressed. This strong reluctance to be realistic persisted, and, from 1936 onwards, the Federal Council had nothing whatever to say on the matter at all, feeling in all probability that it could not conscientiously advocate disarmament or rearmament.

On the outbreak of war in 1939, however, both the Federal Council and the Free Church Council faced the hard facts and quickly made up their minds. In an appeal signed by the Archbishop of Canterbury, Dr. Lang, the Moderator of the General Assembly of the Church of Scotland, and Dr. Bond, the Moderator of the Federal Council, and issued from Lambeth Palace, the Federal Council was committed to these words:

> It is . . . a supreme moral and indeed spiritual issue which is at stake. At all costs for the sake of the world's peace and order, the policy proclaimed by the German Fuhrer must be resisted and overcome. It is based on force. It must be met by a counter force. . . . The only effect of any appeal of non-resistance upon Hitler would have been to encourage him to pursue his way with more ruthless determination.[1]

The Free Church Council sent a message in similar vein to all ministers and Free Churchmen.

We have seen that the outlook of the Federal and Free Church Councils was substantially the same. Strong support was given to the League of Nations; and to other peace organizations such as the World Alliance for International Friendship. Both councils, for well over a decade, maintained an uncompromising policy of disarmament. In both councils about 1935, a division of opinion appeared in relation to the vexed issue of pacifism, and an examination of the debates and resolutions of both councils shows clearly that the pacifist position was rejected. Both councils explicitly, and implicitly by continued support of the League of Nations, declared that after all other means had failed, an international security force might have to be used.

[1] *Baptist Times*, September 21, 1939. The appeal entitled "Christian Citizenship in Time of War" is printed in full.

Bearing these facts in mind, it is difficult not to criticize the Free Church attitude to the world situation, more especially in the middle 'thirties, for lack of realistic vision. To call for continued disarmament at a time when Hitler's intentions were becoming increasingly aggressive is somewhat mystifying, especially after the extreme position of the pacifists had been rejected. Had the Free Churches accepted the pacifist plea, then at least their policy would have been consistent. Once granted the use of force as legitimate under certain conditions, however, then it behoved a practical policy not only to advocate some kind of international security force—as the Free Church Council did—but also to ensure that such a force was adequately equipped to discharge its obligations and to be in a constant state of preparedness. The latter obviously could not be secured without a measure of wise rearmament. How the Free Churches expected an international force to be in a position to enforce the authority of the League of Nations and to uphold its ideals, when all the major powers except the two main aggressors were disarming, is difficult to understand.

An example of this curious indecision and refusal to face unpleasant facts may be seen in two resolutions passed at the Sheffield National Free Church Council in 1933. The first resolution strongly condemning Japan's attack upon China and her refusal to accept the findings of the League of Nations although bound to the League, appealed for the withdrawal of all financial and other support. The second resolution commended disarmament, not merely in an academic manner, but as a practical policy for the international situation. Such indecision and vacillation was calculated to undermine the League's authority and to make it a laughing stock—as indeed it did—the very result which the Free Church Council wished to avoid.

The Free Church reply would have been, no doubt,

that once naked and unprovoked aggression had taken place, and all attempts at arbitration and conciliation had failed, then the League could set about taking steps to assemble and equip a force to chastise the aggressor. Such a policy would have been far too late. The superiority in military might of the aggressors was such that by the time the necessary steps had been taken, the position from the League's point of view would have been well nigh impossible. In other words, the League, with its lack of any power to enforce its authority, simply invited the aggressors to confront it with a *fait accompli*, as Hitler was not slow to see. It was abundantly clear that somewhere Hitler would have to be stopped in the interests of the world community, but the fact remains that the vacillation and indecision of the supporters of the League made ultimate war absolutely certain—again the very thing they wished to avoid.

It is true that it is somewhat unjust to criticize the Free Churches for their inconsistency when the Allied governments, who might have been expected to be more practical, took up more or less the same position along with the majority of their peoples. Perhaps also there is a measure of excuse for the Free Churches when we remember the tension that the discussions concerning pacifism produced in their midst. Although the majority rejected the pacifist position, there remained a minority, which was often influential and eloquent, who would have nothing whatsoever to do with force of any kind whether under League of Nations' supervision or not. Again, it must be borne in mind that in relation to the Boer and Great Wars, general Free Church sentiment had been anti-militarist and prejudiced against any preparation for war. None the less, the inconsistency of the Free Church position remains, and it is the historian's duty to point it out. Much may yet depend on whether we can learn the lesson.

Chapter 13

THE FREE CHURCHES AND THE REVISED PRAYER BOOK

THE controversy over the revision of the Anglican Prayer Book developed during the last years of the primacy of Archbishop Randall Davidson in 1927 and 1928, but the revision was the outcome of long and careful deliberations ever since the findings of the Royal Commission on Ecclesiastical Discipline in 1905 and 1906. These deliberations resulted in a Revised Prayer Book being presented to the Convocations in 1927, whence, by large majorities, the book was commended to the Church Assembly.

The new book permitted the shortening of morning and evening prayer with alternative forms; it increased the number of occasional prayers and gave leave for the priest to employ extempore prayer; it permitted the saying of prayers for the departed and provided for considerable revision of the occasional offices in order to produce more harmony both with liturgical tradition and modern ideas. An alternative form of Holy Communion was included which met a desire to revert to the 1549 Prayer Book. Though many of these alterations were debated at length, the main controversy centred around the vexed question of the Reservation of the Sacrament and, indeed, for all practical purposes, the new book was to stand or fall upon this issue.

The practice of Reservation, which had the authority of the first Reformation Prayer Book of 1549, though not included in the 1552 and 1662 revisions, made it possible for a sick person to receive the Sacrament without a fresh celebration, the elements having been "reserved" from the public celebration. The practice was revived about the middle of the nineteenth century, after some three hundred years of neglect, and it developed by degrees, thus raising the thorny problem of the proper treatment of the reserved elements. The 1549 Prayer Book had stipulated that the priest should administer the reserved Sacrament to the sick as soon as possible, but with the revival of the practice many abuses soon appeared. In 1866, for example, Bishop Thirlwall referred to adoration of the consecrated wafer, and the Roman festival of Corpus Christi being observed by some of the clergy. In 1900, Archbishops Temple and Maclagan forbade absolutely the Reservation of the Sacrament, while in 1911 a Draft Rubric forbade the use of reserved elements for any other purpose than administration to sick and needy folk. Despite the efforts of the bishops to control abuses, however, Archbishop Davidson could write:

> I am awaiting with genuine alarm discussions which may take place in Convocation . . . about Reservation, which would give evidence of defiance on the part of many hundreds of clergy who mean to insist on the right of priests and congregations to insist on the use of the Reserved Sacrament for purposes of devotion (as contrasted with Communion) in a way which would have been not only surprising but repellent to Lancelot Andrewes, or William Laud, or E. B. Pusey or John Keble.[1]

These words need little comment for they clearly show that episcopal and even arch-episcopal authority had failed to prevent abuses in connexion with a usage which was not even in the Book of Common Prayer.

[1] G. K. A. Bell, *Randall Davidson*, 1935, Vol. II, pp. 798f.

In the Revised Prayer Book, therefore, the bishops had to face the question of the Reservation of the Sacrament. That some Prayer Book recognition was necessary was, on the whole, conceded, but the bishops knew full well that they must distinguish sharply between Reservation for the Sick, and Reservation for devotion. The latter was a type of concentrated cultic devotion, as in the Roman Church, implying doctrines regarded as dangerous by Protestants. The development of any cultus of adoration was, in fact, the logical outcome of thinking in terms very similar to the Roman doctrine of Transubstantiation. The bishops, therefore, decided to limit the practice of Reservation by means of rubrics setting forth the purpose and method of the usage. This was straightforward enough in connexion with known sickness and demands which could be estimated in advance, but emergency illness, accident and other emergencies had also to be taken into account. The result was that a measure for Continuous Reservation was included in the Revised Prayer Book in order to secure that no sick or dying person might lack the benefit of the Sacrament, and the practice was placed under the permission and control of the bishops. The rules, furthermore, required the reserved elements to be retained in an aumbry or safe in a place approved by the bishop, except on or above the Holy Table. It was this matter of Continuous Reservation which became the heart of the difficulty in the debates on the new book, for its opponents were not slow to point out that superstitious practices would be inevitable. The bishops, realizing that such objections would be raised, made this sincere effort to define and condition the practice of Continuous Reservation.

The Church Assembly, reassured by the Primate's explicit declaration that the bishops would require obedience to the new rules, passed the book in all three houses by large majorities, and, under the terms of the Enabling

Act, the Revised Prayer Book went forward to Westminster.[1]

The new book was the cause of extraordinary and widespread interest. The question was eagerly debated on all sides, and the press had plenty to say. Pamphlets abounded, objections came from many sides, and there is little doubt that the general view was that the book challenged Reformation doctrine and that, even if it was sound and necessary, many clergy would go beyond it on the road to ritual excess.

The Federal Council and the Free Church Council, in the meantime, had not been passive spectators. In 1926, while the bishops were putting the final touches to the new book, the Federal Council had held a most animated discussion on "The Maintenance of the Reformed Doctrine of the Church and the Sacraments", while the 1926 Assembly of the Free Church Council passed a strong resolution against "Romanizing" influences in the Established Church. In this debate there was a good deal of feeling against the Anglo-Catholics, and Dr. R. C. Gillie set the writing on the wall when he declared that he would be obliged to ask Parliament to reject the new Prayer Book.

The 1927 Federal Council Annual Meeting was dominated by the Prayer Book problem, and the Moderator, Dr. Carnegie Simpson, deemed the subject important enough to devote the whole of his Moderatorial address to it. He reminded his hearers that over the greater portion of the new book almost everyone was agreed, and that its rejection by Parliament might be a disaster to any prospect of peace in the Church of England. Reservation, said Dr. Simpson, was full of error for the reason that the elements were only part of the Sacrament and that the real Presence

[1] The "deposited" Book (thus described because it was "deposited" with the Clerk of Parliament), was not intended to supersede the Book of Common Prayer. Its use was to be optional.

was Christ-in-His-Sacrament. The devotional idea behind Reservation led therefore to an unscriptural and unspiritual localization. Having expressed this basic objection, Dr. Simpson pointed out that the new book guarded against abuses of Reservation, at least in words, by forbidding the elements to be used apart from Communion for the Sick. Reservation was therefore merely extended Communion, and the bishops had been careful not to accept any doctrine implying adoration. The Prayer Book Revision was full of peril, but it was not a denial of Reformed doctrine:

> The real danger lies less in terms of its alternative services and rubrics than in how it will be used and to what it will lead.

The burning question was whether the new book would be obeyed, said Dr. Simpson, and the past record of the bishops in securing obedience could hardly satisfy public anxiety.

With characteristic fairness, Dr. Simpson came to the following three conclusions:

1. The Free Churches should take no action which would injure the peace and progress of the Church of England except on the strongest grounds of faithfulness to truth and duty.
2. It was not possible to say with fairness that the new Book would subvert the character of the Church of England if it was faithfully adhered to as the limit of what was not only permissible but permitted within the Church.
3. It was therefore a matter of fair dealing on the part of the Church of England and a matter of duty for Members of Parliament to see that substantial and sufficient guarantees were given to the nation that the limits would be effectively maintained, should the Book become law.

Dr. Simpson's address has been examined at some

length because it can with much justification claim to be the finest utterance on the matter from the Free Church side. It displays a concern for the Church of England in its troubles, whilst holding on to the main realities of the problem and seeking the most harmonious solution.

The Federal Council had previously received an official request from the Parliamentary Ecclesiastical Sub-Committee to express an opinion on the new book, and after careful and prolonged discussion a resolution was finally agreed upon. This made it clear that the Council could only express the opinion of its assembled representatives and that it had no title to speak, at that moment, for the denominations.[1] Full recognition was accorded the fact that the new book was intended to meet the growing needs of public worship and to limit perilous practices, but grave concern was expressed over the abuses of Reservation in the past. This important resolution in its closing words left the Parliamentary Committee in no doubt as to where the Free Churches stood:

> The Council is of the opinion that the final attitude of large sections of the Free Churches will be determined by the adequacy of the guarantees which it is requisite should be specifically given by the authorities of the Church of England prior to the discussion of the measure in Parliament, to ensure that the Book, should it be allowed to pass, will fix the limits not only of what is permissible but of what is actually permitted in the Church of England.

The Prayer Book Committee of the Free Church Council, desiring to keep in step, also directed special attention to the subject of adequate guarantees. An Evangelical Churchman, Sir William Joynson Hicks, went a good deal further and suggested that the Primate should state that there would be no promotion for clerical offenders. No

[1] Some of which had spoken for themselves in calling for the rejection of the Book.

guarantees were forthcoming, however. The Archbishop and the bishops refused to commit themselves to any methods of discipline.

On December 12, 1927, the Revised Prayer Book was presented to a House of Lords,

> filled from end to end with such a crowd as I can hardly remember seeing there, great animation and interest, and much uncertainty as to how the vote would go.[1]

The Archbishop of Canterbury, who introduced the measure, claimed that the new book would greatly help the work of the bishops. He reminded the House of the representative character of the Church Assembly ("the people really qualified to speak") which had given the new book overwhelming majorities, and he assured his hearers that the bishops intended that the provisions of the book should be obeyed. It was an able and convincing introduction, and the measure was eventually carried by a large majority.

On December 15 the debate in the Commons began before a crowded house which was alive with unusual tension and excitement. The Archbishops were present in the gallery. Dr. Carnegie Simpson, who was also present in the Distinguished Strangers' Gallery, refers to the "astonishing ineffectiveness"[2] with which the measure was presented. The Rt. Hon. W. C. Bridgeman, First Lord of the Admiralty, and a good typical Church of England man, failed to make any real case when introducing the measure. He was followed by Sir William Joynson Hicks, later Viscount Brentford, whose speech, if somewhat superficial, was most effective, and kindled in the House strong Protestant feeling:

> We are asked to go back to medieval times. And why?

[1] J. G. Lockhart, *Cosmo Gordon Lang*, 1949, p. 304.
[2] P. Carnegie Simpson, *Recollections*, 1943, p. 89.

> Because, as the Bishop of Durham has said, the situation has become literally intolerable, because the bishops cannot cope with clergy who take a different view from them and deal with these illegalities. We are asked to bring illegal men into line with the law by altering the law. (*Cheers.*) The Bishop of London has said quite frankly that the new book gives the Anglo-Catholics all they have fought for, for the last forty years.[1]

A cool, detached and reasoned argument against the book came from Sir John Simon, and other speakers followed in similar vein, but the Primate later claimed that the most telling speech of all, so far as votes were concerned, was made by Mr. Rosslyn Mitchell, M.P. for Paisley:

> It was a simply ultra-Protestant harangue with no real knowledge of the subject, but owing its power to a rhetorical presentment of No Popery phrases and arguments of the sort which are to be found in *Barnaby Rudge*, when the Lord George Gordon riots set London aflame.[2]

The sincere and earnest Protestantism of speaker after speaker, and the ineffectiveness of the eagerly awaited defence of Lord Hugh Cecil to stem the tide were other features of this historic debate. The drift was plainly against the book, and when the division came it was rejected by 238 to 205, and the Commons in one night had undone the onerous work of more than twenty years.

In the debates, it became clear that there was a deep distrust of the will, or the power, of the bishops to enforce the new book, and also a feeling that the bishops, after failing to put down certain practices, now proposed to legalize them. Later in December, the Archbishop issued a statement in which he attributed defeat in the Commons to certain avoidable misunderstandings, refused to accept the vote as final, and resolved to reintroduce the measure after modification.

[1] *The Manchester Guardian*, December 16, 1927.
[2] G. K. A. Bell, *Randall Davidson*, 1935, Vol. II, pp. 1,345f.

The leaders of the Church of England were in a difficult position. The new book had received ecclesiastical sanction, it had passed the Lords, and even in the Commons it had received a majority amongst those who were professing members of the Church of England. The parliamentary setback raised the problem of the entire relation of Church and State, and some Anglicans, notably the Bishop of Durham, Dr. Hensley Henson, were in favour of terminating the relationship. Others, realizing that the bishops had miscalculated Protestant feeling in the Commons, urged the Archbishop to remove Continuous Reservation from the book. Others considered that if the principle of Reservation was accepted at all, some measure of Continuous Reservation was necessary, and that it would be too great a surrender to the secular arm to carry out a drastic surgical operation on the new book.

What eventually happened was that the conditions attached to Continuous Reservation were made more definite and rigorous,[1] thus alienating the Anglo-Catholics whilst not really winning the Evangelicals. By April 1928 the amended book passed the Convocations and the Church Assembly with majorities substantially reduced.

Commenting on the amendments in a letter to the *Manchester Guardian*, on January 27, 1928, Dr. Barnes, the Bishop of Birmingham, wrote:

> This revision seems to me gravely inadequate. Little has been done to remove objectionable features or to lessen the misgivings expressed in Parliament. . . . The abuses now associated with Reservation would be impossible if the consecrated bread and wine were not allowed to be reserved within the area of public worship. A motion to prohibit Reservation where worship customarily takes place was nevertheless rejected. Some check to abuse might effectively

[1] For example, elements had to be locked up in a safe and were to be renewed at least once a week. Also the Black Rubric was inserted.

> be made if there were no indication by a lamp or otherwise of the place where consecrated elements were reserved. A proposal to forbid such indication was nevertheless rejected. . . . The aumbry may project from a wall, it may have an elaborate door or canopy, there may be a ledge underneath it on which flowers or candles are placed, a lighted lamp may burn before it and notices that the Church has special sanctity because the "Blessed Sacrament is here reserved" may be prominent. . . . The Commons, almost of necessity, must reject the present proposals.

In the meantime, the Free Churches had been watching events with great interest and vigilance, and on March 2, 1928, a sub-committee of the Federal Council addressed a long letter to the Archbishop of Canterbury, so that the standpoint of the Free Churches might be considered before the final amendments were made. The letter was written in the most friendly spirit and expressed the hope that Reservation would be solely for communicating the sick. Dr. Davidson, in a gracious reply, expressed appreciation of the tone and reasonableness of the Free Church statement and felt that the final amendments would be not unsatisfactory.

In this same month of March the Free Church Council expressed its strong determination to seek the rejection of the new book if the practice of Continuous Reservation appeared in the final form. When the Anglican revisers had finished and the result was known, the Free Churches were forced to act. The Federal Council at a special meeting in May, expressed regret that the final revision did not meet the serious objections raised throughout the country and in Parliament, and that no effective measures had been promised for securing obedience.

> For these reasons the Council holds that the objections which determined the vote of the House of Commons are still valid and therefore urges that Parliament should withhold assent to the Prayer Book Measure 1928.

The truth was that the bishops had seriously underestimated the feeling behind the Commons rejection and they did not appreciate that sturdy English Protestants would not be satisfied with revisions which were described before the Church Assembly as merely for the purpose of removing misunderstanding. The emendations were to satisfy nobody, Anglo-Catholics, Evangelicals, Free Churchmen nor the ordinary observer.

On June 13, 1928, the House of Commons rejected the Revised Prayer Book for the second time by the slightly larger majority of 266 to 220, despite the fact that its supporters were this time more impressive in its defence than in the previous December. Lord Hugh Cecil, the Duchess of Atholl, and to some extent Stanley Baldwin, all made excellent speeches on behalf of the book, but they made little impression upon the Protestant convictions and suspicions of their opponents. Behind the arguments it was again clear that many felt that the bishops could not or would not keep the clergy within the prescribed limits. J. G. Lockhart has put his finger on a vital factor when he claims that one of the causes of the temper of the Commons was the long-accumulating resentment against Anglo-Catholic clergy who had often ruthlessly thrust their ritual upon unprepared country folk.[1] This smouldering resentment now burst into fierce flame in the persons of ordinary English Members of Parliament, especially those from rural areas.

What would the bishops do? The question aroused great interest and speculation all over the country. Constitutionally they were in a weak position, for by the terms of the Enabling Act (1919) to which they had consented, and under which the Revised Prayer Book was submitted, the right of rejection was definitely reserved to Parliament but, undeterred, the bishops declared the "inalienable

[1] J. G. Lockhart, *Cosmo Gordon Lang*, 1949, pp. 308–309.

right" of the Church to formulate its faith and to express it in worship. Accordingly, at the end of 1928, the Revised Prayer Book was published by the privileged presses with a preface in which care was taken to show that the new book could not be regarded as authorized for use in churches. In July 1929 the bishops went a step further and indicated that they would not treat as disloyal any deviations within the limits of the new book. Later in the year, the Archbishop of Canterbury claimed that in the absence of parliamentary authority the bishops must authorize necessary changes in worship on their own responsibility but he forbade the general practice of Continuous Reservation—the clergy should secure the consent of their bishop and their own parish council. Along these lines then, since 1928, dioceses have been administered.

It was only to be expected that the permissive use of the rejected Prayer Book would evoke strong Free Church disapproval, and the prevailing Free Church position is well summarized in the now famous words of Dr. Carnegie Simpson:

> The book, though lawfully rejected, might with impunity and even with episcopal sanction be used. Parliament had eaten the cake but the Church would still have it. Or to change the figure, an umpire, agreed upon the terms of the Enabling Act—which once again I say, the Church had accepted, and under which it had proceeded—had given his decision but the decision was to be ignored. Really this was hardly cricket.[1]

The Church of England was in a painful position. The bishops could hardly take the decision as final and abandon the book altogether, for the self respect and spiritual authority of the Church was at stake, and, after all, a Royal Commission in 1905–06 had recognized the need

[1] P. Carnegie Simpson, *Recollections*, 1943, p. 91.

for some modification of and addition to the Act of Uniformity. As Dr. Temple wrote in 1928:

> The first need is a Prayer Book corresponding to the real spiritual life of the Church. . . . Then it will become possible to check such disorders as still remain. . . .[1]

Again, the bishops could hardly go to the other extreme and openly defy Parliament, although no less a figure than Lord Birkenhead advocated such a course. This view, however, was never seriously entertained by any large group, for it would have entailed the severance of the Church and State relationship in a particularly ungracious and indeed unchristian manner.

The third course, the one which the bishops decided to take, was to depart from the Act of Uniformity by sanctioning the permissive use of the Revised Prayer Book under certain conditions. This kind of thing had been done before, of course, but in this case it was done in face of an explicit refusal of sanction by Parliament. Dr. Lang claims that this course was justified by the success of the new book in the general use of the alternative offices of Baptism and Holy Matrimony.

On the other hand, there is no doubt at all, to use Dr. Carnegie Simpson's phrase, that it was hardly cricket, and the appointment of the Commission on Church and State relationships in 1930 is perhaps one indication that the bishops felt this also, possibly more deeply than is generally allowed. The previous wide prevalence of abuses of Reservation, such as Exposition and Adoration, and the refusal of the bishops to give specific and convincing guarantees that such abuses would cease, made the Free Church position a strong one, for Dr. Davidson had admitted in 1917 that such abuses would have been repellent to the great Anglican divines.

[1] In a letter to *The Manchester Guardian*, January 27, 1928.

Again, the Free Church position was strong because it corresponded with the temper and views of the majority of English Protestants. There is a deep Protestant strain in the English race which is determined, obstinate and quite uncompromising, and the Revised Prayer Book immediately inflamed this deep loyalty in the nation, and the Free Churches played a great part in the struggle by enabling this loyalty to become articulate.

Again, Free Church unity in the matter contrasted very much with the disunity of Anglican churchmen which was one of the chief reasons for the failure of the book to secure the necessary parliamentary sanction. The only evidence of any Free Church disagreement is to be found in a document signed by thirteen members of the Federal Council, supporting the Revised Prayer Book. Dr. Carnegie Simpson, Dr. Scott Lidgett and Dr. W. B. Selbie were the chief "rebels" in this connexion, but generally speaking, the Free Churches put up a united front. They were firm in their conviction that their objections were well founded, and confident that they were speaking not only for themselves but for Evangelical Protestantism as a whole.

It is perhaps necessary to meet the objection which queried the right of the Free Churches to interfere at all in the matter. In the first place, the Parliamentary Ecclesiastical Sub-Committee invited the Federal Council to give its ruling when the book was initially submitted to Parliament. In the second place, it was quite clear that the Archbishop did not resent the Free Church statements. For example, a letter sent from the Federal Council to the Primate in 1928, began:

> We do not need to preface this letter with any justification . . . of the participation of the Free Churches in this national religious question. That came to be accepted in the debates of last year, and was not only explicitly recognized, but even welcomed, both by Your Grace and by the Archbishop of York.

Moreover, the Free Churches had a certain right to act as a trustee of Evangelical Protestantism. They could not stand by in silence and indifference while a new Prayer Book was brought forward which seemed to them to threaten certain aspects of Reformation doctrine. Furthermore, the approach to the Free Churches by the Anglican bishops in the Lambeth Appeal, surely gave the Free Churches the right to state their objections to a measure which threatened to reduce all talk of reunion to a mockery. Indeed, when the Anglicans expressed their readiness to resume the Lambeth conversations in 1931, the Free Churches showed at first a certain hesitancy which was partly rooted in the suspicions engendered by the Prayer Book controversy.

Finally, the Prayer Book controversy revealed the need for a Free Church organization which could speak with unequivocal authority and with all possible speed in an emergency. Theoretically, the Federal Council was created for that purpose, but before it could speak with real authority, it had first to refer to the constituent denominations who might have to consult their assemblies, national and even perhaps local. All this took time, and an authoritative Free Church declaration might take months or even a year or more, and in a real emergency such delay would be quite out of the question. In the matter of the Revised Prayer Book, the declarations of the Federal and Free Church Councils, although not strictly authoritative, were a sufficient indication of the Free Church point of view, the more so because separate denominations felt so strongly on the matter that they published their own views. Moreover, popular opinion, which expressed itself promptly and vigorously, was on the Free Church side, generally speaking, so that little was lost despite the lack of a really authoritative Free Church body.

The Federal and Free Church Councils emerged from

the controversy with honour, for they displayed restraint and an understanding of the deep and complex issues involved, and so helped to avoid what could easily have become a most embarrassing and tragic collision between the Church and the law. It would have been hard to forgive the Free Churches if they had endeavoured to make capital out of the whole unfortunate situation. To their credit they did not.

Chapter 14

ANOTHER LOOK AT EDUCATION

TO all intents and purposes the first World War made an end of Passive Resistance, although the protest was carried on by a number of Free Churchmen. As late as February 1923, John Clifford in the year of his death addressed the Annual Meeting of the Passive Resistance League, but by that time the protest was very much of a spent force.

Mr. H. A. L. Fisher's Education Bill of 1918, while it did not remove the grievances upon which the Passive Resistance movement was founded, was cordially welcomed by the Free Church Council because it represented a considerable advance in the educational system. Among some of its admirable provisions, it improved the salaries of teachers; it created an easier path to the universities by a system of state scholarships and special grants; it set up a single school certificate which was accepted as a basic qualification by all the main professions; it compelled attendance at school between the ages of 5 and 14 and instituted continuation classes up to the age of 18; and it severely restricted the employment of children. Free Churchmen were naturally disappointed that the grievances of the 1902 legislation had not been removed but, none the less, the Act was received with approbation, and even the redoubtable Clifford could say:

> A new ideal of Education has been lifted into sight. The teacher is to be better trained and better paid. The school house is to be healthy and well equipped and the years of

adolescence are not to be allowed to reduce to ruin the good work of children's years.[1]

During the period 1919–39, one of the most interesting developments on the Free Church side was the formation of a Joint Education Committee, composed of representatives of both the Federal and the Free Church Councils. This committee began to operate about the end of the year 1927, and stood, in general, for three main principles:

1. A unity of Educational administration under elected authorities directly responsible to the ratepayers.
2. A scheme for improving religious and moral instruction in all schools provided that freedom of conscience applied to all teachers and scholars, and that no discrimination was made on the grounds of willingness or unwillingness to give or receive such instruction.
3. Opposition to the Right of Entry for denominational purposes into the Council schools.

This committee played no small part in the educational discussions up to 1939, and one of the first things to which it turned its attention was the promotion of biblical and religious syllabuses in order that they might become the basis of common religious instruction, not only in the provided schools but also in the voluntary ones. After 1930 considerable progress was made and most local Education Authorities began to examine them seriously, and increasing numbers adopted them. There was extensive co-operation between the Free Churches and the Anglicans, and Dr. Scott Lidgett, in co-operation with the Council of Christian Education,[2] assisted in initiating an

[1] Sir James Marchant, *Life of John Clifford*, 1924, pp. 135–136.

[2] The Council arose out of meetings between the Youth officers of the main Free Churches. Dr. Basil Yeaxlee was chairman and the Rev. Arthur Hallack, secretary. The Council, a voluntary rather than official organization, accomplished a great deal of valuable work in the matter of persuading Local Education Authorities to adopt Agreed Syllabuses. (The pioneer ones

agreement with the Archbishop and bishops for the improvement of syllabuses and for their use not only in provided schools but also for general instruction—not catechetical—in the non-provided schools.

The year 1931 marked the abortive attempt of Sir Charles Trevelyan, President of the Board of Education, to pass through Parliament his proposal for aid to the non-provided schools. The aim was to raise the school-leaving age to 15 and to provide building grants to meet the extension and adaptation of the premises involved. Sir Charles hoped to secure an agreement by negotiation with the various parties involved, but Free Churchmen maintained stout objections and, in any event, although the Bill passed the Commons, it was rejected by the Lords, and it was not reintroduced under the terms of the Parliament Act. The Joint Education Committee of the Free Churches made it clear that it could only assent to the provision of building grants for denominational schools on the following terms:

1. Such grants should be regarded as emergency measures and should not constitute a precedent.
2. They should apply only to the extension or adaptation of existing schools.
3. Only schools selected by the local authorities should receive such grants.
4. A proportionate financial effort should be made towards the cost of extension by the managers.
5. Agreed Syllabuses should be prepared for use in all such schools, and the instruction should be subject to a conscience clause.
6. The appointment of teachers, and questions of conditions,

were Cambridgeshire and the West Riding of Yorkshire.) The Council might have done much more if the Free Churches had been more generous. I am indebted to Dr. Yeaxlee for this information.

discipline and dismissal in schools receiving grants should be transferred to the Local Education Authorities.

Controversy centring around the first, fourth and last of these conditions prevented agreement between the Free Churches and the Board of Education. It may seem that Free Churchmen were unusually obdurate in the matter, but these objections were in conformity with the declared educational policy of the Free Churches at the time, namely that all schools supported by public money should be under complete public control, and that, in the interests of educational efficiency, the entire system should be unified and all disabilities inflicted on grounds of religious belief upon teachers and scholars, removed.

In February 1936, Mr. Oliver Stanley, President of the Board of Education in Mr. Baldwin's government, introduced his Education Bill into the Commons. Mr. Stanley had adopted the policy of hearing all points of view and then making his own decision. He did not invite the churches to bargain among themselves. He had been constantly informed of the Free Church position, for the Joint Education Committee had appointed deputations which had conferred with his predecessor, Lord Halifax, and in January 1936, Mr. Stanley himself met a number of representative Free Churchmen at the Board of Education, among them being Dr. Sidney Berry, Dr. M. E. Aubrey, Dr. Workman, and Dr. Townsend.

The main proposal of the Bill was to raise the school-leaving age to 15 years in 1939, the delay being due to the need for adapting buildings and training teachers. The Bill provided for certain exemptions, and it authorized Local Education Authorities to provide Emergency Grants up to 75 per cent of the cost of building in connexion with either extension of premises or the building of new schools for the senior scholars.[1] The Bill also proposed to give

[1] These were to be known as "special agreement" schools.

permission to parents to "opt" for their children to receive religious instruction from the Agreed Syllabuses within those denominational schools which received grants. The Bill also proposed to make a distinction within grant-aided schools between "reserved" and "unreserved" teachers. The former would be appointed in consultation with the managers and would give religious instruction according to the Trust deeds. The latter would be appointed solely by the Education Authority and would only give Agreed Syllabus instruction, and that only if trained and willing. Reserved teachers, in general, would be appointed in proportion to the number of scholars who required denominational religious instruction. The Bill left the provided schools untouched, and ensured that in non-provided schools which received the grant, the Local Education Authorities would be more or less in command of the situation.

As in the case of Mr. Fisher's Bill in 1918, the Bill of 1936 represented an undoubtable and appreciable advance, but, none the less, it encountered some opposition. The Free Church Joint Education Committee considered that the building grants should not exceed 50 per cent of the cost, and should not be extended to the building of new denominational schools, because this would mean, in effect, the extension of the dual system of education, to which Free Churchmen in general were opposed. They took the view that if the State was prepared to pay 75 per cent of the cost of new schools, it should be prepared to pay 100 per cent and secure entire control. Again, Free Churchmen considered that in view of the generous provision the appointment of all teachers should be in the hands of the Educational Authorities, and that Agreed Syllabuses should be made compulsory instead of being made permissible upon the request of parents. Considerable uneasiness was expressed at the number of the exemptions allowed in the raising of the age, and fears were expressed that these might defeat the main purpose of the legislation. However, the Joint Education Committee, bearing in mind these criticisms, gave provisional approval to the Bill but:

> would call attention to the fact that the disadvantages of the Dual System of Education which are prejudicial to the educational efficiency of the nation and against which the Free Churches have continually protested, still remain unremedied and call for early legislative action.[1]

Opposition was not confined to the Free Churches. At a representative meeting of education authorities in February 1936, only thirteen out of five hundred voted for the exemptions as they stood. The teaching profession were unhappy about the division of teachers into the somewhat nebulous categories of "reserved" and "unreserved", while the Roman Catholics made it clear that they would hold out for the principle of "only Roman Catholic teachers in Roman Catholic schools".

At the end of May, however, Mr. Stanley's Bill passed the Report stage without a division and it became law later on in the year. The Archbishop of Canterbury's amendment in the Lords, that the building grants should be applicable in certain circumstances to junior denominational schools as well, was ruled out after the Joint Education Committee had expressed itself strongly by means of a letter from Dr. Scott Lidgett to Mr. Stanley. The Roman Catholics supported the measure after certain concessions in the matter of appointing teachers to their schools. It was not, however, what it has often been called, an Agreed Measure, and the Free Churches had occasion to make this clear before very long. On all sides, it had been felt that the series of exemptions was unwise, and it

[1] *The Minutes of the Joint Education Committee,* p. 190. The only known copy of these is at the Congregational Union, Memorial Hall.

is true that in the working of the Act the main aim was hampered by the "beneficial employment" exemption. Practically the whole of the Act was suspended on the outbreak of war in 1939.

In November 1938 a joint deputation of the Federal and Free Church Councils waited on the President of the Board of Education. The Joint Education Committee had been closely scrutinizing the effects and development of the new Act for some time, and this deputation made three requests:

1. The publication of all building schemes and the careful investigation of any objections lodged.
2. Agreed Syllabuses to be the basis of religious instruction in all denominational schools receiving grants.
3. The "reserving" of teachers only in proportion to the number of scholars requiring denominational instruction.

Prior to this, an important letter signed by the President of the Free Church Council, Dr. J. D. Jones, the Secretary, Dr. Scott Lidgett, and the Moderator of the Federal Council, Dr. Robert Bond, was widely circulated and published at the beginning of 1938. This made it perfectly clear that the 1936 Education Act was not an Agreed Measure, and it set forth the main Free Church criticisms of the settlement. The Free Churches, as we have seen, never committed themselves to the approval of the 75 per cent grants for new denominational schools. There had however been a good deal of misunderstanding throughout the country amongst Free Churchmen, many of whom felt their hands to be tied because they wrongly judged the Act to be an Agreed Measure. Frequently they had refrained from opposing what appeared to them to be excessive denominational activity, and this important letter cleared the hesitancy and opened up the way for a more thorough vigilance.

No one can deny that vigilance was required. It was

obviously a great temptation for all the denominations concerned to procure as many new and fine buildings as possible at a quarter of the normal cost, for out of school hours such buildings were available for parochial and social work and the like. As there had been a growing disposition to withhold support from diocesan funds for schools, due to a general feeling that the council schools were doing their work, including religious teaching, special appeals and funds were launched to secure the 25 per cent needed to supplement the 75 per cent grants, and in this way large sums were raised. Not all the applications for grants were well founded. In the Hornsey, Finchley and Wood Green area, the Roman Catholics asked for a new school on the grounds that they could find over 200 scholars, the minimum required by the Act for a senior school being 160. Each of the three Local Education Authorities made independent investigations, and found that they could not agree with the numbers claimed and the application was accordingly rejected. Less careful or more pliable authorities might easily have endorsed the application. It was apparent that the greatest care was required to ensure that new schools were only accepted where absolutely necessary, so as to obviate undue extention of the dual system, and to guard against waste of public money.

In the closing years before the second World War, unofficial conferences had been going on between Free Churchmen and Anglicans on the general subject of religious education. These were strongly supported by the Free Church Council in particular, and Dr. Scott Lidgett played a leading part in the discussions. Eventually a report was published which emphasized the importance of corporate worship and instruction in the Christian Faith, and called for reverent and intelligent study along these lines in all colleges and schools.

This co-operation between Anglicans and Free Churchmen in the matter of religious education and the new spirit of understanding and goodwill that it indicated, went far towards producing a working solution in the realm of education. As long as each side attempted to score off the other, disharmony and resentment were bound to increase, but when both sides by mutual discussion, co-operation and concession, endeavoured to make the best of the prevailing legislation, then the difficulties engendered by the continuance of the dual system of education were lessened considerably. The co-operation of the churches in maintaining and improving religious teaching in schools by the production of progressive syllabuses, and the growing tendency of the Anglican Church to commend them as a basis of religious instruction in the denominational schools as well as the council schools, was an enlightened and welcome advance. This did much to end the scandal of sectarian division, and accordingly contributed to educational progress.

The 1944 Education Act of Mr. R. A. Butler was in the nature of a religious compromise. Mr. Butler, by reason of his commendable readiness to receive deputations, and to consult with the representatives of the churches, went a long way towards reconciling conflicting interests. The Free Church Federal Council throughout the negotiations upheld the principle for which Free Churchmen had contended so staunchly down the years, namely that the use of public money should be publicly controlled. The Act has by no means solved the educational problem and the dual system is still a central feature on the educational landscape, but the Act was none the less a step forward. Briefly, it offers the managers of Church schools a choice of becoming an Aided School in which half the cost of reconstructing the premises to meet the demands of the Ministry will be met by the State, the managers retaining control of school and staff, or becoming a Controlled School financed entirely by the State but with Church representatives retained on the Board of Managers. In all schools religious instruction is statutory and in all except aided schools such instruction is based on the agreed syllabus. The fact that, before the Bill was passed, over four hundred education authorities were using these syllabuses is irrefutable evidence of their quality and remarkable vindication of Free Church endeavours in the anxious years after 1918.

Much was hoped for from the Butler Education Act. Much has been achieved: more awaits those who with consecrated minds and hands will pass through the doors it opened to bring to man's search for truth the touchstone of Christ.

Chapter 15

THE TWO COUNCILS UNITE

WHEN the Federal Council was formed in 1919 there was no trace of any suspicion that the days of the Free Church Council were numbered. Right from the start of the time in which the two councils lived side by side, it was accepted that the Free Church Council had its own invaluable and indispensable part to play by reason of its "popular" voice and its extensive local network. The Federal Council might take authoritative decisions and be a more official body, but it would need the Free Church Council network if it was to be other than a mere name to the Free Churches. The more official matters appertaining to the Free Churches, such as reunion negotiations, were left, apart from expressions of opinion, to the Federal Council. The Free Church Council realized that it still had its own part to play in stimulating the Free Church and indeed a wider conscience, and by giving immediate and popular, though unofficial, expression to Free Church opinions, as well as undertaking a vast amount of practical religious and social work by means of its network of local Councils.

The Free Church Council in the last twenty years of its existence not only persisted in existing alongside its more official sister organization, but succeeded in quickening and deepening its life and work. As Dr. S. W. Hughes rightly pointed out in 1932, the Free Church Council was the only body which united the Free Churches in effective co-operation without affecting or limiting their autonomy or liberty. The Federal Council did not diminish the need for Free Church Councils, for as long as autonomous denominations remained in being, the Free Church Council was necessary in order to express quickly and effectively Free Church opinion on matters of spiritual and social well being.

As late as 1935, Dr. Rushbrooke, after wide and devoted presidential visitation, had no hesitation in testifying to the marked progress of the older Council. Everywhere he found eager self-examination and scrutiny of methods, and a general spirit of expectancy. New councils continued to be formed and old ones revived, and confidence and energy abounded on all sides. The Annual Assemblies during the period were vigorous and superbly organized, and drew the customary large crowds. Indeed, they were easily the largest Free Church meetings of the day. Free Churchmen and the public came to expect, as if by right, an imposing array of speakers and they were seldom disappointed. The Archbishop of York, Dr. Lang, in 1921, the Bishop of Manchester, Dr. William Temple, in 1922, Sir Oliver Lodge in 1924, Sir Norman Angell and Lord Halifax in 1934, and the Prime Minister, the Rt. Hon. Neville Chamberlain in April 1940, a few weeks before the dramatic events of the following month swept him from office, are just a few examples of some of the eminent public figures who graced the Council platforms during these years.

The major activity on the local scale was undoubtedly evangelistic, stimulated in the first place by Dr. Clifford's famous Personal Evangelism campaign,[1] maintained by the Rev. Tom Sykes working as an official Free Church Council Missioner as Gipsy Smith had done, and later by the inspiring and successful work of Dr. F. W. Norwood and the Rev. Lionel B. Fletcher, both of whom accepted

[1] This campaign was largely under the guidance of Dr. Clifford. A series of a dozen booklets was widely circulated and the details urged upon every Free Church minister. *Free Church Chronicle*, June, 1921, pp. 54–58.

appointments as evangelists under Free Church Council auspices. Vigorous temperance work and extensive united devotional services vied closely for second place to evangelism.

The Federal Council, on the other hand, distinguished itself by its efficient and statesmanlike handling of the Free Church side of the Lambeth conversations and the Revised Prayer Book controversy. Other less spectacular but important work was accomplished. The Council enthusiastically supported the Personal Evangelism Campaign, and constructive conferences on evangelism were a feature of Federal Council discussions during these years. In 1930, the Federal Council, after a stirring moderatorial address by Dr. Charles Brown, set up a strong committee to explore the possibility of Free Church union. Two years later, Hugh Martin, in a brilliant address on "The Unity of the Free Churches", gave to this committee a vigorous "shot in the arm", and this resulted in a theological commission to study the issues involved. This commission reported back at intervals and was still in existence at the outbreak of the second World War, but little actual progress towards union was made, and the matter was more or less eclipsed by the attention centred on the proposals to unite the Federal and the Free Church councils. One of the most important functions of the Federal Council was its representation of the Free Churches on national and other important occasions, and the Moderator soon became a public figure. In 1935, Dr. Sidney Berry, as Moderator, read the lesson in St. Paul's on the occasion of the Thanksgiving Service for the Silver Jubilee of King George V. It fell to the lot of Dr. Berry in his term of office to take part in the Memorial Service arranged by the British Broadcasting Corporation on the Sunday following the death of King George in January 1936.

In connexion with the Coronation in May 1937 the

Federal Council sent a letter to the Coronation Claims Committee asking that the Free Churches in the person of the Moderator of the Federal Council should take part in the Coronation Service in Westminster Abbey, and Dr. M. E. Aubrey in his moderatorial address in September 1936 made this scarcely veiled reference:

> A national occasion should be national and not sectional, and it cannot be national so long as only a part of the nation is represented there . . . so long as the nation upon occasions desires religious expression to be given to its deep feeling, the Free Churches as a very large part of the nation, should have a worthy part.

The argument was very much an over-simplification of the complex religious and ecclesiastical issues involved, but its reception in Free Church circles showed that there was some support for the Moderator's claim that the Established Church should not assume a monopoly of the service in which the King of England was crowned Sovereign of *all* his subjects. On November 28, 1936, the Archbishop of Canterbury put the other side of the case in a letter[1] to Dr. Sidney Berry. He pointed out that no analogy existed between the Coronation Service and the Silver Jubilee Thanksgiving Service for the simple reason that the former followed, in words and acts, centuries-old traditions and precedents. On these grounds and those of the ordered sequence and unity of the service, it was impossible to allot a place for the Free Churches. A joint committee of the Federal and Free Church Councils wisely decided not to pursue the matter at a time when the nation was plunged into the throes of the Abdication crisis.[2] The Primate, however, largely by dint of his own

[1] A reprint of this letter can be seen in *The Report of the Federal Council*, September, 1937, pp. 16–17.

[2] King Edward VIII abdicated on December 10, 1936. During the events leading up to this fateful decision, the Free Churches were consulted by the government.

endeavours, secured invitations for six Free Churchmen[1] to walk in the Coronation Procession and to have seats within Westminster Abbey reserved for them. The Moderator also took part with the Primate and the Moderator of the Church of Scotland in a Broadcast Service on the Sunday prior to the Coronation, and was privileged to read the lesson in St. Paul's on the occasion of the Empire Day Service at which the King and Queen were present. The Moderator in 1938, Dr. M. E. Aubrey, represented the Free Churches at the Lord Mayor's Banquet and had the unique honour of addressing both Houses of the Convocation of York—the first occasion on which a Free Churchman had ever done this.

The Moderator, then, became a public figure, and in a real sense he was the Free Church counterpart of the Archbishop of Canterbury, in the public eye. He could, by virtue of the constitution of the Federal Council, claim to represent and speak for the Free Churches as no other man could, yet it should be noted that the President of the Free Church Council also walked in the Coronation Procession and received invitations to be present on other great public occasions. This indicated a certain amount of confusion in the minds of the authorities of the Church of England and the State as to who was the authentic Free Church figurehead.

The Federal Council, however, never captured the popular imagination of the rank and file of Free Churchmen to the extent that the "unofficial" Free Church Council did. In the nature of the case, it was largely precluded from doing so because it was, for the most part, a body confined to the leaders of the Free Churches meeting once a year as officially appointed delegates, and a body

[1] The Moderator of the General Council, the President of the Free Church Council, and the elected "heads" of the Baptist, Congregational, Methodist and Presbyterian denominations.

which was strictly limited by its constitution. It never met outside London and it never staged the popular rallies which its sister organization did. Indeed, all its efforts in the direction of publicity were restricted with the result that, except to the leaders of the Free Churches, it was little more than a name. This is not inconsistent with the claim that the Moderator was a national figure. He was prominent and in the public eye on a number of formal and ceremonial occasions, but that is quite different from saying that the Federal Council was widely known. It is a definite fact of history that it was not, and in 1936, the Federal Council showed its deep concern by circulating widely a booklet setting forth the work and purpose of the Council in the hope of capturing the imagination and energies of more Free Churchmen. This consciousness on the part of the Federal Council members that they had not secured the recognition which was desirable, coincided with other impulses which were working in the direction of one Free Church organization which would ally denominational authority with popular appeal; but before we consider that important event, there is an interesting story connected with the relations between the two Councils.

When the Federal Council came into being in 1919 there was more or less general recognition that both councils had distinctive rôles to fulfil. Free Churchmen recognized a dual need, firstly for an organization backed by denominational authority and capable of acting and negotiating for the Free Churches on specific matters; and secondly, for one which, without reference to denominational authority, could quickly rally and express the popular opinion of Free Churchmen in addition to uniting locally for Christian action. Theoretically, this seemed satisfactory, the more so because a body for liaison and co-operation between the two councils was quickly set up, namely, the Nexus Committee consisting of members of both bodies. Opinions and memories differ, however, as to how much actual co-operation took place. Both Dr. Scott Lidgett and Dr. Sidney Berry[1] maintained that the Nexus Committee never accomplished much and that for the most part the two councils went their own ways. On the other hand, Dr. S. W. Hughes claimed that there was a good deal of useful co-operation. There is no doubt that some co-operation did exist. For example, it was a joint committee of the two councils which drew up and published a provisional reply to the Lambeth Appeal in September 1920, and the more important statement, "The Free Churches and the Lambeth Appeal" in March 1921. There was, after 1927, a Joint Education Committee comprising representatives of both councils, and this did most important work. At the time of the Coronation, a joint committee drew up an Order of Service for use in the Free Churches, and another joint committee examined the Archbishop's letter to Dr. Berry in 1936 on the matter of Free Church representation in the Abbey. These are examples of joint action at the national or headquarters level, but they did not materially affect the vast network of local Free Church Councils over the country. That is where co-operation seems to have broken down or where, to say the least, much more might have been accomplished.

In 1920 the Free Church Council committed itself to the following words:

> Whatever the future relations of our Council may be with the Federal Council, we shall always be able to supply the machinery by which the concerted plans of the denominational representatives may be carried into effect.[2]

[1] Interviews with Dr. Scott Lidgett at 27 Tavistock Square, London, on October 17, 1950; Dr. Berry at Memorial Hall on November 7, 1950; and Dr. Hughes at Baptist Church House on November 14, 1950.

[2] *Free Church Year Book 1920*, p. 34.

The possibilities of such action, however, do not seem to have been explored to any serious extent, and the divergency of opinion between Dr. Berry and Dr. Scott Lidgett on the one hand, and Dr. Hughes on the other, regarding the question of co-operation, is perhaps due to the fact that the former was thinking of action which extended beyond national headquarters, while Dr. Hughes may have been referring to the useful work accomplished at that level.

Throughout the twenty years when the two councils ran concurrently, constant dissatisfaction was expressed with the relations between them. As early as 1921, the Nexus Committee was investigating the possibility of uniting the two councils, but to no avail. In 1926, in response to a request from the Baptist Union, the matter was reopened, but the time was considered to be inopportune because of certain impending changes among some of the federated churches. In 1931, the President of the Free Church Council, the Rev. Dr. Griffiths Jones, urged that pressure should be brought to bear upon this problem because:

> both these splendid institutions . . . are now unquestionably far too independent of one another, to the great loss of both and the Christian public.

As a result, the Nexus Committee was enlarged and met more regularly to examine the way forward.

All this raises the question as to whether there was any truth in the popular criticism that rivalry existed and that relations were not always cordial between the two councils. Many prominent Free Churchmen, of course, actively supported both organizations. Men like Dr. Scott Lidgett, Dr. J. D. Jones, Dr. Rushbrooke, Dr. Carnegie Simpson, Dr. Garvie, Dr. Workman and Dr. Selbie, to mention only a few, were to be found wholeheartedly working in both councils without any thought of inconsistency. There was clearly no need of rivalry or jealousy as long as both councils adhered to their own rôles.

Only when one or the other tried to usurp the other's rôle could relations have become strained. Did this actually happen? The Free Church Council, in the nature of the case, was unable to play the part of the Federal Council, for no amount of simulation could give it the necessary official standing. There does seem to have been, however, a feeling amongst some members of the Free Church Council, chiefly among those who did not serve on the Federal Council, that the Federal Council was elected merely for *ad hoc* purposes, and that it should not express itself upon matters for which it was not specifically commissioned. Some felt that the Federal Council was presumptuous and "poached on Free Church Council preserves".[1] This accusation seems to rest on a misunderstanding. True, the Federal Council did derive its power to act from the denominations, and it was commissioned in specific matters, but there was nothing in its constitution to prevent it discussing any matter and rendering an Advisory Report to its federating members. The Free Church Council could hardly claim a monopoly of the live issues of the day! There was no danger of the Federal Council supplanting the Free Church Council as the popular voice of the Free Churches for the simple reason that its discussions did not receive wide publicity, but were reported mainly for the information of the denominations. If Free Church Council members seriously believed that the Federal Council was exceeding its powers they could have raised the matter in their own denominational assemblies. That no such action was ever taken indicates that we may safely acquit the Federal Council.

[1] These are the actual words used, in my presence, by one of the leaders of the old Free Church Council.

Official relations between the councils were cordial, and no matter what certain Free Churchmen might say in unguarded moments, there was never any actual ill feeling between the two bodies. There was, no doubt, criticism and comment, but it was never malicious and it never estranged the two councils. The fact that so many prominent Free Churchmen actively supported both bodies was a more than adequate safeguard.

It was only natural that a certain confusion should exist in the country over the parallel existence of two bodies both claiming in their own way to represent the Free Churches. Free Churchmen who appreciated the distinction, no doubt found it hard to understand that Anglicans, or the Home Office, or the Lord Chamberlain or the general public should be puzzled, but the fact that there were *two* organizations was enough to mystify the ordinary onlooker who had neither the time nor the inclination to delve into the intricacies of the situation. The question must often have been asked by the public and by government departments, "Which Council represents the Free Churches?" and "Does the President of the Free Church Council, or the Moderator of the Federal Council represent the Free Churches on a national occasion?"

The issue was, of course, most prominent in the fourth decade of the century when a number of great national occasions took place. Dr. S. W. Hughes and Dr. Henry Townsend[1] both agree that considerable confusion did exist. Dr. Sidney Berry, on the other hand, claims that the confusion has been much exaggerated. Here again are divergent views.

Human nature is such that some confusion must have existed. The distinction between a popular organization and an authoritative one would not be easily appreciated by people outside the Free Churches. The fact that on

[1] Henry Townsend, *The Claims of the Free Churches*, 1949, pp. 313f.

many notable occasions, invitations were sent both to the Moderator of the Federal Council and the President of the Free Church Council suggests that Canterbury, the Home Office and the Lord Chamberlain were not sure whom to invite and therefore, very naturally, decided to play safe in case offence might be caused. On the other hand, when a speaker was required to represent the Free Churches officially in a broadcast service, or to read a lesson in St. Paul's, it was always the Moderator of the Federal Council who was invited. This supports Dr. Berry's implication that someone did appreciate the distinction in influential circles. The amalgamation of the two bodies in 1940 settled the issue once and for all.

By 1923, the Nexus Committee had recognized that the ideal was one united Council combining the authority of the one with the freedom and wide influence of the other. Why then was the fusion not achieved until 1940? A number of reasons combined to cause the delay.

Firstly, it was judged inopportune to press for the union at a time when important changes were imminent within Methodism, and when the Presbyterian Church of England was watching closely the events which led up to the union of the Church of Scotland and the United Free Church of Scotland. Both Methodists and Presbyterians were therefore preoccupied and so unlikely to bring to this matter as much attention and enthusiasm as they might otherwise have done.

Secondly, a number of Free Churchmen, some of them influential, considered that the distinctive rôles of the two councils could best be fulfilled by two separate organizations. As late as 1936, the Moderator of the Federal Council, Dr. M. E. Aubrey, could claim that the existence of both was necessary.

Thirdly, and this reason was strongest in the early days of the Council when memories of the first twenty years of the century were fresh, many members of the Federal Council felt that they should be more cautious than the Free Church Council. They recalled that the latter, rightly or wrongly, had fought the General Election of 1906 for the Liberals, and as a result of this and other memories they were inclined to regard the older Council with a certain amount of suspicion. It seemed to some to be too much concerned with issues not specifically religious, and many tended to regard the Federal Council as a superior body brought to birth by the deficiencies and failings of the older body. There was a good deal of prejudice and a great amount of ignorance involved in this attitude, but in fairness it must be said that it was based on a sincere desire to keep the Federal Council free from any entanglements which might discredit it.

Fourthly, the pressure of outside events, such as the Lambeth conversations and the debate over the Revised Prayer Book, meant that the fusion of the two councils received less attention than it otherwise would have done. A fifth reason was that the denominational secretaries and leaders were most reluctant to depute any more authority to a body outside themselves. The weakness of the Federal Council had been that its maximum speed was that of the slowest denomination. A chain is as strong as its weakest link. The Federal Council had been the limit to which the Free Churches would go in the direction of union. The denominational leaders therefore viewed with apprehension for many years the possibility of a new and greater Council which would have wide support. It might, for example, attempt to lead a crusade against the jealously guarded ramparts of denominational individualism.

In the latter half of the fourth decade, however, the demand for one united Council became more and more insistent. Events in Europe were beginning to produce a spirit of unity among the people of Britain[1] which was bound to translate itself into all manner of relationships. Moreover, the discussions and experiences of Free Churchmen on the joint committees set up by the two councils finally showed that the existence of two organizations was becoming more and more of an anomaly, and that there was no real reason why the essential characteristics of each could not be combined in one body. Both lacked effective authority, and the respective leaders began to realize that a united Council would be more successful in a number of directions. Clearly, it would be a gain to have one organization claiming to express and represent the convictions of Free Churchmen on matters in which they could act together, and it would, moreover, dispose entirely of the confusion and misunderstanding in public circles.

On September 16, 1937, the first link was forged in the chain which was to bind the two councils together, when the special General Purposes Committee of the Free Church Council sent a resolution to the Federal Council urging immediate steps to explore the possibility of one united Free Church organization. A Joint Committee was duly set up and it held its first meeting in January 1938. Dr. Henry Townsend in an important contribution said:

> At the present time neither the Anglican Church nor the Government can communicate or negotiate with one united Free Church authority. When grave moral issues are confronting our nation, our Free Church convictions should be uttered by a united, authentic voice. It should be possible for us to co-operate quickly with the leaders of the Anglican Church and equally possible for us to make our views known

[1] Some will contest this, but men began to feel, however inarticulately, that we in England must stick together at all costs. Hence the frequent and often savage outbursts against men like Oswald Mosley. It helps to explain too the amazing spirit after Dunkirk. Actually this was the culmination of something which had been there all along.

to the Government of the country and the Press. . . . We desire a Council constituted as authoritatively as possible and capable of safeguarding Free Church interests as emergencies arise.[1]

In a long and interesting discussion which ensued, speeches in support came from Dr. Scott Lidgett, Dr. F. W. Norwood, Dr. Rattenbury and many others, and eventually the following resolution was carried, moved by Mr. R. Wilson Black and seconded by Dr. J. W. Ewing:

That it is desirable that there should only be one National Council representing the Free Churches of this country, and that a small sub-committee be appointed to draw up a scheme and to present it to this Committee at as early a date as possible.

Some Free Churchmen were opposed to the idea, and Mr. J. A. Leckie, the Treasurer of the Federal Council, put their objections forcibly in a letter to Dr. Berry. He claimed that both councils had separate functions which did not overlap, and he considered that Free Church Council spontaneity and initiative would be lost in an official body which would be prevented from being a "live" organization.

By January 1939 the sub-committee had done its work so well that a more or less settled scheme resulted, and the Federal Council in this same month approved the proposals, rejecting *en route*, it is interesting to note, a plea for full organic union by the Rev. E. Aldom French. In March 1939, the Free Church Council at its Annual Assembly also endorsed the Federation proposals and the scheme then went on to receive, during 1939, the provisional approval of the denominational assemblies. By the end of July 1940 the proposals in their final form had been accepted by all concerned with practical unanimity

[1] *Special Committee Minutes*, the only copy of which is at Memorial Hall. Many of the pages are unnumbered.

and considerable enthusiasm. The stage was set for the final act.

The new Constitution attempted to combine the advantages of each Council. One hundred and twenty-five representatives were to be chosen by the denomination in agreed proportions, and a further seventy-five by popular vote at the Annual Free Church Congress. The Council was to meet not less than twice a year, and was to work throughout the year by means of a General Purposes Committee of twenty-five members. The local Free Church Councils were to be incorporated and renamed Free Church Federal Councils. In addition to the proposed twice yearly councils, arrangements were made to hold an Annual Free Church Congress consisting of the members of the Federal Council and one representative from each local Council. The Constitution clearly aimed to preserve the chief characteristics of both the uniting bodies. It was an adventure in comprehension and aimed at making everyone feel at home.

In July 1940 the Moderator of the Federal Council and the President of the Free Church Council issued a Call to Prayer. It was the last joint action of the two councils and it was a much-needed summons. The nation was in a desperate, and to many it seemed a hopeless, position. Belgium and Holland had been invaded and quickly overrun by the German war machine. France had fallen—a victim of her traditional enemy and her own traitors. The gallant British Expeditionary Force had been snatched from the jaws of death on Dunkirk's never-to-be-forgotten beaches, by an apparent miracle. The English Channel was the last unstormed bastion beyond which the people of this island stood together in a unity of spirit and purpose never before or since experienced, and resolved to sell their lives dearly. It was perhaps one of the most fateful and tense moments in the whole history of our world.

Prayer was a vital reality to millions of Englishmen in a way that it had never been before, as they waited for the cruel onslaught which they knew must come.

It was at such a tremendous moment that the Free Church Federal Council was born, for the final act of union took place in the early afternoon of Monday, September 16, 1940, in the Baptist Church House, Southampton Row, Holborn. An air raid was in progress and the skies were full of violence and terror. The Battle of Britain was at its height and England stood at one of the most fateful hours of her long history. All over the country, permeating every class and creed, a matchless spirit of unity prevailed. Devotion, sacrifice, comradeship, and high endeavour were no mere empty clichés but magnificent realities. What an hour in which to live and what an hour in which to come to birth!

In Southampton Row that afternoon many hearts were proud and glad that a great new chapter of Free Church history had opened at such a moment. Many Free Churchmen felt that perhaps this was the finest hour, not only of England in her rôle as the sole bastion of freedom, but for the Free Churches too as they faced the new challenge and opportunity which that September afternoon presented to them.

Chapter 16

WHITHER THE FREE CHURCHES?

THE Free Church Council movement, as a whole, has been one of the important features of Free Church life. It was essentially a religious movement with its main activities and interests evangelistic throughout. Judgments to the contrary have usually been related to episodes or phases of the movement and not to the total picture which displays a consistent and regular missionary emphasis, at times so consistent and regular as to be unspectacular and in danger of being overlooked when other and more dramatic events were taking place.

It is no exaggeration to say that some of the finest and most instructed evangelism in the history of Christianity in this country emanated from the Free Church Council, and, significantly, not as a series of spasmodic efforts but rather as a sustained enterprise. The Great Simultaneous Missions were examples on the grand scale of a purpose which belonged to the very *esse* of the movement. Even at the height of the Education controversy and in the midst of political tensions, evangelism did not merely persist but actually increased.

The movement is also significant because of the practical experience of co-operation and teamwork which it fostered among Free Churchmen. The limited Methodist reunion in 1907 and the much larger one in 1932 owed more than is generally allowed to the valuable links which had been forged between the various uniting bodies in local Free Church Councils and upon their platforms. It is impossible constantly to work and pray with people without growing to appreciate and understand them more. Again, the Free Church Council contributed to the general atmosphere which made possible the Lambeth Appeal. The fact that the Council was gradually making an end of exaggerated isolationism within the Free Churches contributed to the 1920 "climate" quite apart from the considerable co-operation and understanding which developed between the Council and the Anglicans during the exigencies of wartime. The Free Church Council was an adventure in unity and, as such, imparted strength to the general spirit of unity among Protestants which has been a feature of our national life, and indeed of wider spheres, during the last forty years or so.

Another important aspect of the movement has been its social conscience. The Free Church Councils accomplished much social relief work, and strongly opposed social evils in the national life. The Federal Council too, showed a concern for social justice, although its witness and work was limited in that it did not possess local organizations. The motive behind all social activity, whether it was relief work, opposition to the brewers, to gambling or Sunday cinemas and the like, was religious. It was an attempt, however faulty one may deem it, to translate Christian principles into daily life, and such work went on whatever government was in power, although Free Churchmen in the early part of the century entertained hopes that the Liberals would see the problems in much the same light. It is true that much of this social activity had its limitations. In relation to problems such as Gambling, Drink, Sunday Observance and Immorality, it was largely negative in its attitude, consisting rather in a succession of "Thou shalt not" actions than in a positive and integrated policy. From some points of view it was a treatment of external symptoms with little real attempt to sympathize or understand. Many will therefore condemn the Council action as naïve and ineffective, not without cause, but it should be remembered that there does come a point where a halt must be called before any positive policy can operate. The main defect of Council action in these matters was that energies seemed to be concentrated on the negative emphasis almost to the exclusion of positive policies.

The original motive behind the Council movement was closely connected with the Grindelwald conferences at the beginning of the last decade of the nineteenth century, when the Council pioneers decided that any immediate steps towards reunion must leave the Anglicans out of the reckoning. Charles Berry and Hugh Price Hughes decided that a useful, and indeed an essential first step, would be to promote the closer unity of the Free Churches. Thus the Free Church Council came into being, and the pioneers proclaimed positive Free Church principles. The negative names "dissenter" and "nonconformist", although they have lasted on, certainly began to fade, and "Free Churchman" and "Free Churchmanship" came into currency. The Free Churches became conscious of their part in the visible Church Catholic, and this partly explains the emphasis in the early years of the Council upon the teaching of Free Church principles.

Into this long overdue process of the re-education of the Free Churches there suddenly burst the events of 1902, the period of the Education controversy, and subsequently the struggle against the House of Lords, and though the evangelism of the Council and all its varied work went on unabated, none the less these events constituted, in a very real way, an interruption in the evolution of the movement.

It is difficult to see how the Council could have avoided participation in the strife of those years, for Free Churchmen, in general, smarted under a sense of injustice which, to us living in a world of far greater problems and tensions, may seem exaggerated, but which to them—and indeed to the Anglicans—was one of the biggest issues on the horizon of that day. Any judgment on the events of those years is faulty unless it allows for the enormous change in the religious atmosphere. At any rate, the Free Church Council became, as Dr. Scott Lidgett has said:

> . . . the protagonist in an embittered strife with the Church of England and the Roman Catholics, and immersed in a political campaign which of necessity assumed the form of a close alliance with one political party.[1]

The Council leaders honestly believed that such political action as they took was justified on religious grounds, and the accusation of being a political caucus came strangely from the Church of England with its own decided political interests. If the Council ranged itself behind the Liberals, no one can dispute the unequivocal support given to the Tories by the Anglicans. The accusation came from some Free Churchmen as well, but the Council never lost its soul and its central purposes were never extinguished or crippled by the pressure of contemporary events. Circumstances did conspire to give to the Council the appearance of a political caucus, but it was never organically related to the Liberal Party in any way.

Political questions often merge into moral ones, and Christianity, if it has any message for the common life of men, should rightly and readily be concerned with such questions. The Church cannot live in an air-tight compartment and, in the last analysis, Christianity has more to fear from those sections of the Church which shut themselves away from municipal, national and imperial affairs than from those which seek, however imperfectly, to translate faith into action on the battlefield of human

[1] J. Scott Lidgett, *My Guided Life*, 1936, p. 184.

endeavour. Dr. Dale maintained that Christians should enter such spheres only as consecrated individuals and that the Church should remain aloof, but it is surely true that an army is always a better fighting force than isolated guerrillas. The latter may do much harm and strike many blows, but they can never win a campaign. They have a nuisance value only. The battles are won by well-led, well-disciplined and well-equipped soldiers fighting as units. The Free Church Council believed that certain legislation was wrong and opposed to the principles of justice and freedom, just as in 1906–10 it regarded the House of Lords as the champion of privilege and favour. The Council believed that the only effective way of dealing with such regrettable situations was by means of fresh legislation. At that time, the Liberal Party seemed to be the only body likely to improve matters. Therefore the interests of justice and freedom, surely intimately related to the heart of the Kingdom of God, could best be served *in those specific circumstances* by supporting the progressive party. We may disagree with the method but we must commend the purpose.

After the Great War, the Free Church Council did no more political campaigning. With the rise of the Labour Party to a strength sufficient to challenge the Liberals—with the advent, in other words, of new Radicals—the Free Church Council largely withdrew from the political arena. Opinions differ as to whether this has been a good or a bad thing. Certainly during the last thirty years or so, Free Church influence upon local government and public life has declined and the nonconformist conscience has practically disappeared. A gulf has grown and is still growing between the Free Churches and the common people. From all points of view this is regrettable, and both the Free Churches and the national life have suffered. The split in and the subsequent collapse of the Liberals, with the rise of Labour as the main alternative to Toryism, found the Free Church Council divided in political outlook, with some suspicious of the Left, others too progressive for the Right, and others able to find a political home in one or other of the two main parties.[1]

The simplest explanation of the Council's political inactivity after 1918 is that the decline of the Liberals and the nonconformist conscience were simultaneous because of a simple process of cause and effect, but this is a patent over-simplification. In or about 1900 thousands of Free Church Council supporters were Unionists. Many developed Liberal sympathies in the years that followed because of specific grievances against Tory policies. They were Liberals because of the pressure of events and at the dictates of conscience. When the pressure was relaxed or when the issues involved seemed less important, what more natural than that many should turn to other political colours which they had worn in earlier years, or to colours which after the Great War appealed to them more? Such indeed was the case. After 1918 many Free Churchmen became Conservatives, some turned to the new Radicals, while others remained convinced Liberals. This three-fold division might well have been much the same even if the Liberal Party had not collapsed. This division also explains the decline in Free Church Council influence upon municipal and national life. Henceforward the Council was never sufficiently unanimous on social and political matters to wield the kind of influence it had done in the first fourteen years of the century.

The events of 1902 and the years that followed constituted, however, an interruption in the wider evolution of the Council movement. It was left to one of the great

[1] e.g., Dr. Clifford, Dr. Orchard and the Rev. Henry Carter gave platform support to Labour programmes, and many Free Churchmen found themselves drawn to the new Radicals.

Free Church statesmen of this century to rediscover the original vision which had inspired the pioneers. J. H. Shakespeare pleaded for a new step forward, not so much out of dissatisfaction with the Free Church Council, but because he recognized that its founders had intended it to be, not an end in itself but an intermediate stage on the road to a closer alignment or union of the Free Churches. The Federal Council, which was the result of Shakespeare's vision and energy, was quite definitely the offspring of the older Council and marked a real stage in the evolution of the movement as a whole. Some regarded its birth as directly due to the fact that the Free Church Council was played out and discredited. Had this been the case, the Free Church Council would hardly have supervised and promoted the birth of an organization intended to render its own existence superfluous, nor would it have been able to perpetuate itself for a further twenty-one years with no little virility and success. The Federal Council was born because of the recognition that, valuable though the rôle of the Free Church Council was, there was an urgent need for a more authoritative body constituted by direct denominational representation. Thus it was recognized by both Councils that each had its distinctive part to play, the older body providing the outlet for the popular and unofficial voice of the Free Churches as well as continuing its laudable activities on the local scale, the new body dealing with matters remitted to it by the Free Churches. So until a new stage in the evolution of the movement dawned, both Councils maintained parallel existences.

The Federal Council quickly established itself and won wide respect by its responsible and competent handling of the Free Church side of the Lambeth conversations, and later by its statesmanlike behaviour over the Revised Prayer Book controversy. The Free Church Council on the other hand continued to accomplish a great amount of good through the local Councils, and to make a considerable impression with its popular Annual Assemblies. Constant efforts were made to bring the two councils together, and when they did eventually unite, the union took the form of a comprehensive attempt to preserve the valuable features of each Council, which is a substantial testimony to the importance of the rôle each endeavoured to fulfil during the years 1919–40.

What were the failings of this great movement? The chief criticism of the Free Church Council was that it lacked authority. Hugh Price Hughes had faced this problem in 1894 and decided that in the initial stage of Free Church unity it was more important for delegates to come together as Free Churchmen than as denominationalists. Consequently, the Council was constituted by delegates from the local Councils instead of from the denominations as such. Events justified this important decision, for the Free Church Council certainly transformed the prevailing "climate" in the Free Churches and ushered in a new era of co-operation and fellowship. It is doubtful whether a similar degree of success would have been achieved had the Council been composed of official delegates. It was precisely because the Council met without denominational badges that it achieved so much in the great cause of unity.

None the less, it remained a popular and unofficial voice, and, as such, was incomplete. Hugh Price Hughes no doubt considered that as the Council was to be but an intermediate stage on the road to closer union, the problem of due authority could be faced at the next stage. Lack of authority cannot therefore be termed a defect because it was deliberately decided at the outset that it should be unauthoritative. Whatever faults that lack of authority displayed, no one can dispute that the Council did prepare the ground for the Federal Council by giving to Free

Churchmen in liberal measure that valuable experience of fellowship together which was the essential prerequisite of a more authoritative organization.

Perhaps a more valid criticism of the Free Church Council is that it took so long—some twenty-seven years—before it gave birth to its offspring, but it was not entirely its own fault that it was so long "in labour". The pressure of important and compelling external events interrupted its development and forced it into years of strife. The original vision was dimmed for a while, and it took a visionary and a statesman—a remarkable combination in one person—of the calibre of J. H. Shakespeare to urge the movement on to self-fulfilment. Some blame must be apportioned to the Council, however, for the impression it gave of revelling in violent controversy. This was not true of the movement at its best, but extremists are found in every camp, and some Free Church Council members sometimes overstepped the bounds of moderation and responsibility, and critics were not slow to use the weapons thus placed conveniently in their hands. Charges of irresponsibility and immaturity were sometimes levelled at the Council, and these were doubly dangerous because of the element of truth within them, but scientific judgments must be related to the total picture and not to one sharp feature.

The chief criticism of the Federal Council is significant because it not only explains why the Free Church Council so easily maintained a parallel existence but also suggests that Hugh Price Hughes possessed a good deal more foresight than many credited him with in 1894. The Federal Council machinery, hard though it worked and successful as it was in more than one direction, was nevertheless cumbersome. In the nature of the case it had to be because it was dependent through its Constitution upon denominational sanction. The delegates were elected and commissioned by, and responsible to, their own denominations. They were therefore much more cautious than their brethren in the older Council. The Free Church Council could quickly put its finger on the pulse of Free Church feeling, to sum it up and disseminate it by methods of popular expression. Perhaps it was not always cautious or accurate, but, generally speaking, it does not seem to have been very wide of the mark. The Federal Council, on the other hand, was responsible to the denominations who might approve or reject its findings. This involved considerable delay in putting a fully authoritative Free Church policy in the field. The Federal Council was also addicted to the practice of referring subjects to committees of its own which would report back perhaps a year later at the Annual Meeting. No doubt there was often good reason for this, but the system was patently cumbersome and involved a delay which, in a real emergency, the Free Churches might be able ill to afford. The Revised Prayer Book controversy demonstrated this deficiency. As it happened, the overwhelming strength of both Free Church Council and public feeling coincided with the views of the Federal Council so that little was lost, but the matter showed that a body with more authority than the Federal Council was necessary if the Free Churches wished to express themselves officially and speedily.

The Federal Council, then, was handicapped by constitutional shackles, and though it made a considerable name for itself in its twenty-one years of existence, it might have been much more effective had the Free Churches trusted it with more authority, as indeed they might well have done in view of the competent and responsible statesmanship which it displayed.

The union of the two Councils in 1940 to form the present Free Church Federal Council was hailed with great jubilation, and its supporters entertained extensive hopes of the work it might do. It endeavours to combine the popular nature of the Free Church Council with the official authority of the old Federal Council. The extensive network of local Councils now comes under the wing of the Free Church Federal Council, and this marks an important step forward in that an authoritative Free Church body can now express itself effectively on the local scale. Broadly speaking, the executive power rests in the hands of officially appointed denominational representatives. The Annual Congress, the successor of the old Free Church Council assembly, is for the most part made up of representatives from the local Councils. The popular voice of the Congress is really in an advisory capacity and the last word lies with the denominational representatives.

Since 1940, no one can dispute that the Federal Council has done much for the Free Churches in a number of directions. It has watched over Free Church interests with vigilance and efficiency. It has won increasing recognition and appreciation in many a government office. It has shown itself to be experienced, competent and responsible in the administration of common Free Church affairs and the defence of Free Church interests. It is quite beyond argument that if the Council ceased to exist, the Free Churches, of necessity, even if only on the one issue of negotiation with government departments, would have to create another body of a similar nature. It is high time that the Free Churches acknowledged their debt to Tavistock Square. To take only one example, the amount of money that the Federal Council has saved the Free Churches in matters of administration and the like, warrants an immediate review of the present level of financial support.

It is doubtful, however, whether the Free Church Federal Council has so far justified the great hopes which greeted it. The great stimulus of the national unity in that fateful September of 1940 made it easy to believe that a great new era had dawned for the Free Churches, and that in the new and wonderful atmosphere sacrifice and generosity would open up the way for a really vital experience of unity.

Alas, it was not to be. The stimulus has long since disappeared and the present Council, almost sixteen years later, finds itself in much the same general position, in relation to the matter of authority, as the old Federal Council did. Basically the difficulty is a simple one. The vision which possessed Charles Berry and Hugh Price Hughes, and later J. H. Shakespeare, that Free Church Federation was to be an expression in structural terms of the positive and the catholic nature of fundamental Free Church principles, has been dimmed. Generally speaking, support for the Federal Council by individuals and denominations alike is regarded much more in terms of an "optional" extra, very much subordinate to denominational loyalties, than in terms of a majestic, scriptural and catholic Free Churchmanship.

Behind this again is the obstinate belief—still a hardy perennial, one suspects—that our own denomination is really the true Church. We will work with others, but on our own terms and only up to a point. Let us beware of making God in our own image and attempting to canalize His grace into the shallow channels of our own understanding. There were those in Isaiah's day who made their own gods with their hands and carried them around as grievous burdens. Isaiah has great sport with them in certain passages, and the majesty of his vision makes it all look so pathetic and tragic. In the twentieth century, the problem is much more intricate and subtle. Free Churchmen are in no danger of such crudity, but perhaps we can fairly be charged with sustained attempts to reduce the great and majestic to the narrow and petty. Certainly, the vision of Grindelwald makes much of our churchmanship pathetic and puny.

Many Free Churchmen feel, however, that developments in the ecumenical movement, resulting in the British and the World Councils of Churches, have raised the question of the position or even the need of a lesser grouping such as the Federal Council. It is true that there has been much useful co-operation in certain directions between the Free Churches and the Church of England within the British Council of Churches, but it is equally true that in the matter of wider reunion something suspiciously akin to stalemate has now been reached. It is over thirty-five years since the Lambeth Appeal and there is still relatively little progress to record apart from the welcome growth in understanding and the crystallization of the main obstacles. The strong "confessional" emphasis of the major Free Churches seems to indicate fairly definitely that the present stalemate is likely to continue.

A realistic policy therefore must begin, as Charles Berry and Hugh Price Hughes saw so clearly long years ago, from the simple fact that the best contribution the Free Churches can make to the cause of reunion is to come, as quickly as possible, much closer together. There is much truth in the claim that the British Council of Churches cannot begin to realize much of its potential strength until the Federal Council is really powerful. There is an urgent need for a united, and not a piecemeal, Free Church witness and contribution within the wider framework.

At the same time, it is abundantly clear that the necessary spiritual conditions for an actual union of the Free Churches do not, at the moment, exist in large enough measure. It is not just a question of assenting to an acceptable scheme even allowing for the moment that one could be found to surmount the many denominational obstacles. Before actual union can become a real possibility, the Free Churches must be set on fire with a burning spiritual constraint in the matter.

There are certain straws in the current which suggest that the tide is slowly turning in that direction. There are, for example, increasing numbers within all the Free Churches to whom our denominational barriers mean considerably less than they did to our fathers and do to us, and this is not by any means solely due, as some scornfully claim, to an inferior spiritual experience or to that tolerance which is fathered by indifference. A generation is growing up within our Free Churches, whether we like it or not, who may yet surprise us by their insistence on essentials in the interests of the salvation of a fast dying world. The great acts of loving sacrifice and generosity, of which we seem incapable, could yet be possible for them, and the tides of history appear to be on their side. Those who direct Free Church affairs—the safe, the influential and the experienced men—will be ill advised to emulate King Canute, for tides cannot be turned, especially when they are propelled by that Divine Spirit which works in and through and yet so greatly transcends all our divisions.

Free Churchmen who move from one area to another usually find it comparatively easy, when occasion demands, to discover a spiritual home and useful service in a Free Church of another tradition. Any working minister has ample evidence of this as he handles his incoming and outgoing transfers. Some good souls are shocked at the ease with which Baptists and Methodists and Congregationalists and Presbyterians can settle down in each other's fellowships. There is, of course, nothing to be shocked about, only very often we are too proud to admit it.

Economic considerations will force us more and more in the same direction as we attempt to minister to the new centres of population. It is manifestly absurd to suppose that the denominations as such are in a position to keep abreast of this vast and frightening problem. Separately we simply do not possess the resources, and even if we did, the secular authorities would continue to classify us, and rightly, as Free Church, and assign one site only. The church which takes up the site must therefore cater for Free Churchmen generally, and it is reasonable to expect it to make certain adjustments or modifications. It is estimated that the population of the world increases by over 2,000 every hour, while the Christian population increases by four. If those figures have any relevance at all to us in our situation, then it is time to stand together and pool our material and spiritual resources. How are we to possess the land? There is an obvious answer which could be a real possibility for our children, but no one, God forgive us, seems willing or able to face it. It is time to re-examine our position as separate denominations as we hear Christ calling to us from the midst of human need.

What is the first step? Charles Berry, Hugh Price Hughes and J. H. Shakespeare told us long ago that there is an evolutionary growth in this business of coming together. It is time we listened to them again. We must not set our target too far beyond practical possibilities, for that is merely to invite perhaps a disastrous reaction. A horse can be taken to the water but he cannot be forced to drink, but if a thirst is produced within him then the chances are that he will be glad to see the water. We must aim, first of all, at making Free Churchmen thirsty for union, and the first step on that delectable road cannot but concern the instrument which Berry, Hughes and Shakespeare have bequeathed to us.

No one is content with the present functioning of the Free Church Federal Council. Its leadership has not always been what it might be. It has on occasions lacked imagination and inspiration, and it has preferred the valley to the mountain-top in its objectives. Too often it has emulated certain of its ancestors in its preoccupation with negatives, but the fault does not, by any means, lie entirely within itself. The Federal Council is what the Free Churches have made it or allowed it to become, but its potential remains immeasurable and its challenge to spiritual adventure a clarion call. The Free Churches owe much to its work, but it means relatively little in their life and thought generally, and Free Church leaders either will not or cannot make proper use of the weapon so conveniently placed in their hands. Attempts to increase its authority are usually suspect from the outset and are quietly, decently but ruthlessly destroyed by an influential opposition whose vision leaves much to be desired.

How can the Free Churches expect to face and to shoulder the weighty tasks and problems of wider reunion if in face of this preliminary challenge and adventure they remain indifferent and aloof? Words of A. Victor Murray spring to mind:

> The Free Churches . . . expect the nations of the world to achieve without the grace of God that which the Churches with the grace of God are unwilling to attempt, namely, to lay aside their sovereignty for the sake of the common good.[1]

The Free Churches give every appearance of being satisfied with themselves as they are. If this is true, then it is our greatest condemnation, for we are no longer worthy to be matched with this momentous hour. It surely belongs to the genius of our position within the reformed tradition that we are "free" to adapt ourselves to the pressures of life, and to allow God's Spirit to modify our forms as His Purpose requires. To which is our allegiance to be given—the overall and imperative needs of the Kingdom or the jealous patrolling of our denominational fences? Increas-

[1] *British Weekly*, April 3, 1952.

ing difficulties and pressures are likely to compel us to face the issue sooner or later. Pray God it will be sooner.

Let us then send and give our best and bravest to the cause of Free Church Federation as the next step on the road so splendidly driven through sixty changing years. Let the Federal Council lift our eyes to bold and shining horizons, for there are increasing numbers of Free Churchmen who have had their fill of cautious and timorous counsels. May the spirit of apostolic adventure and enthusiasm light up our hearts and energize our hands, and may Berry, Hughes and Shakespeare live again. There are thousands waiting to follow them.

From the sensitiveness that shrinks from everything,
From the stolidity that is pleased with anything,
And from the apathy that is touched by nothing,

Good Lord, deliver us.

(STUART BLACKIE)

APPENDIX

a. OFFICERS OF THE NATIONAL COUNCIL OF THE EVANGELICAL FREE CHURCHES

PRESIDENTS

1896. The Rev. Hugh Price Hughes, M.A. (*Wesleyan*)
1897. The Rev. J. Monro Gibson, M.A., D.D., LL.D. (*Presbyterian*)
1898. The Rev. Dr. John Clifford. (*Baptist*)
1899. The Rev. Dr. Alexander Mackennal. (*Congregationalist*)
1900. The Rev. Dr. Charles H. Kelly. (*Wesleyan*)
1901. The Rev. J. G. Greenough, M.A. (*Baptist*)
1902. The Rev. Dr. W. J. Townsend. (*Methodist New Connexion*)
1903. The Rev. James Travis. (*Primitive Methodist*)
1904. The Rev. Dr. F. B. Meyer. (*Baptist*)
1905. The Rev. Dr. R. F. Horton. (*Congregationalist*)
1906. The Rev. Dr. J. Scott Lidgett. (*Wesleyan*)
1907. Professor J. Rendel Harris. (*Quaker*)
1908. The Rev. Dr. David Brook. (*United Methodist*)
1909. The Rev. Evan Jones. (*Welsh Calv. Methodist*)
1910. The Rev. Dr. J. H. Jowett. (*Congregationalist*)
1911. The Rev. Dr. Charles Brown. (*Baptist*)
1912. The Rev. Dr. Thomas Mitchell. (*Primitive Meth.*)
1913. The Rev. Alexander Connell, M.A. (*Presbyterian*)
1914. The Rev. Dr. F. Luke Wiseman. (*Wesleyan*)
1915. The Rt. Hon. Sir Joseph Compton Rickett, P.C., M.P. (*Congregationalist*)
1916. The Rev. Dr. J. H. Shakespeare. (*Baptist*)

1917. The Rev. Dr. W. B. Selbie. (*Congregationalist*)
1918. The Rev. George Hooper. (*United Methodist*)
1919. The Rev. A. T. Guttery. (*Primitive Methodist*)
1920. The Rev. Dr. F. B. Meyer. (*Baptist*)
1921. The Rev. Dr. R. C. Gillie. (*Presbyterian*)
1922. The Rev. S. Chadwick. (*Wesleyan*)
1923. The Rev. F. C. Spurr. (*Baptist*)
1924. The Rev. Dr. A. E. Garvie. (*Congregationalist*)
1925. Dame Elizabeth Cadbury, M.A., J.P. (*Quaker*)
1926. The Rev. Dr. H. Elvet Lewis.
(*Welsh Congregationalist*)
1927. The Rev. W. Conrad Balmer. (*United Methodist*)
1928. The Rev. Professor A. S. Peake, D.D.
(*Primitive Methodist*)
1929. The Rev. Dr. Thomas Phillips. (*Baptist*)
1930. The Rev. Dr. J. Alfred Sharp. (*Wesleyan*)
1931. The Rev. Dr. E. Griffiths Jones. (*Congregationalist*)
1932. The Rev. Dr. James Reid. (*Presbyterian*)
1933. The Rev. James Lockhart. (*Methodist*)
1934. The Rev. Dr. J. H. Rushbrooke. (*Baptist*)
1935. The Rev. Dr. F. W. Norwood. (*Baptist*)
(later regarded himself as a *Congregationalist* when at the City Temple)
1936. The Rev. Dr. J. E. Rattenbury. (*Methodist*)
1937. The Rev. James Colville, M.A. (*Presbyterian*)
1938. The Rev. Dr. J. D. Jones. (*Congregationalist*)
1939. The Rev. Dr. J. W. Ewing. (*Baptist*)
1940. The Rev. Walter H. Armstrong. (*Methodist*)

SECRETARIES

The Rev. Thomas Law. (*Wesleyan*) 1896–1910
The Rev. Dr. F. B. Meyer. (*Baptist*) 1910–1920
The Rev. Thomas Nightingale.
(*United Methodist*) 1920–1931

The Rev. Dr. S. W. Hughes. (*Baptist*) 1932–1940

The Rev. Dr. J. Scott Lidgett served as Honorary Secretary from 1914–1940.

TREASURERS

Sir Robert W. Perks. (*Wesleyan*)	1897–1910
George Cadbury. (*Quaker*)	1897–1923
Evan Spicer. (*Congregationalist*)	1897–1905
Sir J. Compton Rickett. (*Congregationalist*)	1905–1913
The Rt. Hon. T. R. Ferens, M.P. (*Wesleyan*)	1910–1930
Sir R. Murray Hyslop, J.P. (*Congregationalist*)	1913–1934
Sir Beddoe Rees, M.P.	1923–1930
George Shrubshall, J.P.	1930–1933/4
R. Wilson Black, J.P. (*Baptist*)	1933–1940
A. E. Glassey. (*Congregationalist*)	1935–1937/8

b. OFFICERS OF THE FEDERAL COUNCIL OF THE EVANGELICAL FREE CHURCHES

MODERATORS

The Rev. Dr. J. H. Shakespeare. (*Baptist*)	1919–1920
	1920–1921
The Rev. Dr. J. D. Jones. (*Congregationalist*)	1921–1922
	1922–1923
The Rev. Dr. J. Scott Lidgett. (*Wesleyan*)	1923–1924
	1924–1925
The Rev. Dr. David Brook. (*United Methodist*)	1925–1926
The Rev. Dr. P. Carnegie Simpson.	1926–1927
(*Presbyterian*)	1927–1928
The Rev. Dr. A. E. Garvie.	1928–1929
(*Congregationalist*)	1929–1930
The Rev. Dr. Charles Brown. (*Baptist*)	1930–1931
The Rev. J. T. Barkby. (*Primitive Methodist*)	1931–1932

The Rev. Dr. W. Lewis Robertson. (*Presbyterian*)	1932–1933
	1933–1934
The Rev. Dr. Sidney M. Berry. (*Congregationalist*)	1934–1935
	1935–1936
The Rev. Dr. M. E. Aubrey. (*Baptist*)	1936–1937
	1937–1938
The Rev. Dr. Robert Bond. (*Methodist*)	1938–1939
	1939–1940

SECRETARIES

The Rev. Dr. C. Anderson Scott. (*Presbyterian*) Minute Secretary	1919
The Rev. Dr. W. Lewis Robertson. (*Presbyterian*)	1919–1935
The Rev. Walter H. Armstrong. (*Methodist*)	1920–1940
The Rev. Dr. J. H. Shakespeare. (*Baptist*)	1921–1925
The Rev. Dr. Sidney M. Berry. (*Congregationalist*)	1936–1940

TREASURERS

Sir Walter Essex. (*United Methodist*)	1919–1934
Mr. William Mallinson, J.P. (*United Methodist*)	1919–1935
The Rev. Dr. W. Lewis Robertson. (*Presbyterian*) (Assistant)	1934–1935
J. A. Leckie, M.P. (*Presbyterian*)	1935–1938
The Rt. Hon. Ernest Brown, M.P. (*Baptist*)	1938–1940

When the Free Church Federal Council was formed in 1940, the Rev. Walter H. Armstrong was the first Moderator. The Secretary was Dr. S. W. Hughes, and the Treasurers were R. Wilson Black, J.P., and the Rt. Hon. Ernest Brown, M.P., with Dr. Scott Lidgett and Dr. S. M. Berry as Honorary Secretaries.

INDEX